MOVE LIKE WATER

Bruce Lee's Timeless Lessons

Find Your Flow, Build Your Power, Express Your Authentic Self,

Live with Impact

By

PRADEEPKUMAR K PADMANABHAN

★ ★ ★ ★

Table Of Contents

Foreword 9

Preface 13

Part I: 23

The Way of the Dragon – Understanding Bruce Lee 23

1. The Boy Who Danced Between Cultures 25

    1.1 Early Life in Hong Kong and America 26

    1.2 Lessons in Cultural Fluidity 27

2. The Artist in the Fighter 31

    2.1 His Love for Philosophy, Acting, and Martial Arts 32

    2.2 Integrating Art and Self-Expression into Life 35

3. A Life of Fire: Triumphs and Tragedies 39

    3.1 Injuries, Discrimination, and Setbacks 41

    3.2 Resilience and Reinvention 44

Part II: 47

The Core Lessons – Bruce Lee's Philosophy for Growth 47

4. Be Like Water 49

    4.1 Adaptability and Fluid Thinking 51

    4.2 Stories from Real Fights and Acting Choices 53

5. Hack Away at the Unessential 59

5.1 Minimalism in Thought, Training, and Life 60

5.2 Decluttering Your Inner and Outer World 64

6. Express Your Authentic Self **69**

6.1 The Journey from Imitation to Innovation 71

6.2 Building Your Unique Identity 74

7. Discipline Over Motivation **81**

7.1 Daily Training and Commitment 82

7.2 Mastery Through Consistent Effort 86

8. Fearless Living **91**

8.1 Courage in Confrontation and Career 92

8.2. How to Confront Your Inner Limitations 96

9. The Warrior Mindset **103**

9.1 The Balance of Calm and Power 106

9.2 Dealing with Failure, Criticism, and Chaos 109

Part III: **115**

The Application – Bruce Lee's Wisdom for Modern Life **115**

10. Mind Like Water: Mindfulness and Focus **117**

10.1 Presence in Action 120

10.2 Meditation and the Martial Artist's Mind 124

11. Move with Purpose: Career and Goals **129**

11.1 Pursuing Excellence, Not Fame 133

11.2 Defining Success on Your Terms 137

12. Train Every Day: Habits and Rituals **143**

12.1 The 10,000 Kicks Principle 147

12.2 Designing Your Daily Growth Practice..............................150

13. Live with Impact: Influence and Legacy............................**155**

13.1 Leadership Through Character 159

13.2 Building a Legacy Through Self-Mastery 162

14. The Tao of You: Crafting Your Growth Path **167**

14.1 Journaling Prompts, Exercises, and Actions.......................172

14.2 Creating Your Own Philosophy of Living 176

15. Bruce Lee Lives On: Modern Icons Inspired by Him..........**183**

15.1 Living the Way: Modern Legends Who Embody Bruce Lee's Spirit.188

15.2 You as the Next Torchbearer 193

Appendix..**199**

Bruce Lee Quotes by Theme...199

Resources & Further Exploration 201

Timeline of Bruce Lee's Life...207

Acknowledgements **213**

About the Author..**215**

Disclaimer **217**

May I Ask You For A Small Favor?...**219**

FOREWORD

This isn't just a book about Bruce Lee.

It's a call to awaken what's ancient within you.

For those of us who grew up in the era of Bruce Lee—watching his films, reading his words, absorbing his presence—he was more than a martial artist. He was the pulse in our childhood training, the fire in our practice, the spark that shaped how we saw strength. We moved from admiring his speed to honoring his wisdom, from fists of fury to the mind that forged them. Bruce Lee didn't just fight—he *thought*, he *felt*, and he *refined* the warrior's path.

In my journey across the world as a teacher of martial arts, I've met grandmasters who carved their name into history, and I've worked with students whose hearts burned brighter than their belts. Through them, I've come to believe this: martial arts is not about domination, but transformation. The warrior's way leads not to conquest, but to peace. To wisdom. To love.

Pradeepkumar embodies this evolution. I had the honor of coaching him during the Enlightened Warrior's Power program under Success Gyan. He didn't just attend—he *lived* it. Disciplined. Reflective. Authentic. This book is the echo of that commitment. It doesn't just speak of Bruce Lee—it channels his essence and invites *you* into the arena.

You'll find stories that cut deep, ideas that linger, and moments that stir your sleeping spirit. Whether you're a martial artist or a seeker of self, you'll find something here—a sentence, a scene, a surge—that reminds you of who you truly are.

When you close this book, don't walk away.

Stand up. Stretch.

Find a form. Learn a kata.

Find a heavy bag. Throw a punch.

Honor the warrior ancestors in your bloodline.

Awaken the mentor within.

The next generation is watching.

With deep respect to my students and my masters—

"Please... teach me."

Aaron M. Huey

United States Martial Arts Hall of Famer

International Warrior Trainer

Author of The Four Prime Archetypes: Why We Do What We Do

PREFACE

"Absorb what is useful, discard what is not, add what is uniquely your own."

- Bruce Lee

Bruce Lee was not merely a martial artist, actor, or philosopher—he was a force of nature. A seeker. A creator. A transformer. He defied expectations, questioned limitations, and broke free from rigid systems—whether in fighting, film, or philosophy. He was not interested in conformity; he was driven by authenticity.

This book is not just a tribute to Bruce Lee's life—it is an invitation.

An invitation to explore how one man's disciplined, creative, and fearless way of living continues to ripple through time, inspiring individuals across every walk of life. Bruce Lee's wisdom, forged through both triumph and tragedy, speaks directly to the challenges we face today: identity, purpose, freedom, fear, and self-expression.

He taught us that martial arts is more than combat—it's a metaphor for life. Every challenge is a sparring partner. Every failure is a training session. Every success is a moment of flow. And growth? Growth is the art of learning to move like water—adaptable, intentional, and powerful.

In these pages, you'll walk through the key moments of Bruce Lee's journey. You'll discover the philosophy behind his movements, the depth behind his words, and the wisdom behind his discipline. You'll see how his mindset has influenced modern icons—and how it can shape your own evolution.

This book is especially written for the next generation of students, professionals, creators, and warriors—those who dare to dream, question, and live with impact. It will help you reflect, awaken your spirit, and push forward with clarity and conviction.

Let this be your dojo—not of kicks and punches, but of principles and presence, of authenticity and action.

Because in a world that often teaches you to conform, Bruce Lee's message is loud and clear:

Be yourself, fearlessly and fully.

Why Bruce Lee?

In a world that often forces people into boxes—based on profession, background, belief, or identity—Bruce broke every mold. He didn't just teach us how to fight; he taught us how to live. With intensity, presence, purpose, and passion.

A Life Larger Than Combat

Bruce Lee's real battle wasn't just in the ring or on screen. It was against:

- Cultural stereotypes

- Self-doubt

- Physical limitations

- Societal norms

- And even the boundaries of knowledge itself

He took on these battles with a rare blend of discipline, creativity, and inner stillness. That's why his teachings aren't just for martial artists—they're for anyone who wants to become the strongest version of themselves, mentally, emotionally, physically, and spiritually.

A Teacher for the Modern Soul

We live in a time where distractions are plenty, purpose is diluted, and identity is constantly questioned. In such a world, Bruce Lee's voice cuts through the noise:

- *"Be like water."*

- *"Hack away at the unessential."*

- *"Knowing is not enough, we must apply."*

- *"Do not pray for an easy life. Pray for the strength to endure a difficult one."*

These aren't just quotes. They're life principles—each one forged in the heat of real struggle, failure, and victory.

The Vision Behind This Book

This book is not a biography. It is a bridge—between Bruce Lee's timeless lessons and your daily life. Whether you're a student, a leader, an artist, an entrepreneur, or simply a human being trying to evolve—this book brings you closer to the Bruce Lee within you.

In his short life, Bruce Lee lived more authentically and fully than most people do in a hundred years. The fire he lit still burns—not just in dojos or cinemas, but in the hearts of those who dare to grow, create, and stand tall.

This book is for those who seek growth with depth.

Who want to move through life with power, peace, and presence.

And who are ready to train not just the body, but the mind and spirit.

Reflection: The First Kick That Hit Me Wasn't Physical

I still remember the first time I saw Bruce Lee—not in a dojo, but on an old TV screen. The movie was *Enter the Dragon*. During my school days, I wasn't so good at English. I didn't fully understand what was happening in the plot, but one thing was clear: this man was different. He moved differently. Spoke differently. Carried something within him that was far greater than muscle.

At first, I was drawn in by the speed, the sharpness, the elegance in motion. But what stayed with me—long after the credits rolled— wasn't a fight scene. It was a moment when he paused, looked into the camera, and said, *"Don't think. Feel."*

It was such a simple line. But it hit me like a punch I didn't see coming. Because, with time, I realized—I had been doing the opposite all my life.

I was overthinking everything. My studies, my future, my worth. I wanted to get everything "right." I wanted approval, safety, certainty. But Bruce—he wasn't looking for any of that. He moved from a place of freedom, of inner knowing, of trust in his own being.

That was the moment Bruce Lee stopped being just a martial artist to me. He became a mirror—one that showed me my fears, my hesitation, and more importantly, the possibility of breaking through them.

Years later, as I walked the path of guiding others in personal growth, I returned to Bruce again and again. His philosophy helped me build not just strategies for success—but a mindset rooted in clarity, authenticity, and courage.

Even today, when I feel stuck or uncertain, I ask myself:

"What would Bruce Lee do?"

The answer is never about fighting. It's always about flowing.

A Personal Journey Inspired by Bruce Lee's Living Philosophy

I did not write this book as a tribute to a martial artist. I wrote it as a gift to anyone who has ever felt stuck, constrained, or misunderstood—yet knew deep inside that they were made for more.

Bruce Lee wasn't just a fighter. He was a philosopher in motion. A teacher who never stopped learning. A bridge between East and West. A soul who refused to be boxed, labeled, or tamed.

I first realised Bruce Lee's teachings in a moment of internal struggle. I was navigating a period of confusion in my personal growth. Despite success on the outside, I felt incomplete on the inside.

I was searching—not for more information, but for transformation.

That's when I truly discovered Bruce—not just the man who moved fast, but the man who *thought deeply*. His words cut through the noise. His actions reflected alignment. His principles, though rooted in combat, applied directly to life, leadership, clarity, courage, and freedom.

As a coach for engineers, a seeker of inner clarity, and a student of spiritual living, I began applying Bruce's philosophy in a very practical way. Not to throw punches, but to break through mental blocks. Not to perform, but to express. Not to follow a system, but to create my own.

This book is a collection of the most powerful lessons I've drawn from Bruce Lee's life, teachings, and spirit—and how I've applied them (and helped others apply them) in the real world.

It's a journey of inner engineering. Of turning resistance into rhythm. Fear into fuel. Identity into authenticity.

My vision for this book is simple:

- To remind you of the power already within you.

- To give you clarity, not clutter.

- To offer not a system, but a spark.

Bruce Lee once said:

"The great mistake is to anticipate the outcome of the engagement; you ought not to be thinking of whether it ends in victory or defeat. Let nature take its course, and your tools will strike at the right moment."

Let this book be your mirror, your compass, and your companion—as you shape a life of clarity, courage, and conscious action.

Let's grow.

Let's flow.

Let's be like Bruce.

How to Read and Apply This Book

Turning Bruce Lee's Wisdom into Your Growth Practice

This book is not meant to be read in a rush.

It's not a one-time read. It's a companion for your journey—whether you're an engineer, a creative, a leader, or a seeker of personal excellence.

Bruce Lee lived his philosophy. Every movement, every word, every silence reflected deep inner alignment. That's what this book aims to help you build—not just knowledge, but *inner application*.

Here's how to get the most out of it:

1. Read One Chapter at a Time

Each chapter is crafted around a core idea from Bruce's life. Don't binge. Let one principle sink in before moving on. Even a few pages a week can shift your awareness.

2. Reflect Deeply

At the end of each chapter, pause. Ask yourself:

- How does this apply to my current life or work?

- What's one situation where I can try this today?

Reflection turns knowledge into growth. Make it personal.

3. Practice the Principle

Whether it's "being like water" in a conflict, or "hacking away at the unessential" in your schedule—choose action over intention. Don't wait to be perfect. Start where you are.

"Knowing is not enough, we must apply. Willing is not enough, we must do." — *Bruce Lee*

4. Write Your Own Notes

Use the blank pages or a separate journal. Note your interpretations, challenges, breakthroughs. Over time, this book will evolve into your personal growth playbook.

5. Revisit When You Feel Stuck

Bruce's wisdom is timeless. When life throws confusion, self-doubt, or stress your way—open any page. Let it guide you back to your center.

6. Share What Resonates

Growth multiplies when shared. Discuss what you're learning with a friend, a colleague, or your team. You'll be surprised how many people around you are also seeking clarity and flow.

This is Not Just a Book. It's a Mirror.

You won't just learn about Bruce Lee—you'll learn about yourself.

His way was not to give answers, but to awaken your inner teacher.

Read slowly. Reflect honestly. Practice courageously.

That's how you'll make this book truly yours.

PART I:

THE WAY OF THE DRAGON –

UNDERSTANDING BRUCE LEE

1. The Boy Who Danced Between Cultures

Before he became a legend, Bruce Lee was just a boy—restless, curious, and caught between worlds. Born in San Francisco, raised in Hong Kong, and shaped by both Eastern tradition and Western freedom, Bruce was never fully one or the other. He danced between cultures, refusing to be boxed in.

Where others saw conflict, he saw connection.

Where others followed tradition blindly, he questioned deeply.

Where others copied, he created.

He moved with the grace of a dancer, the spirit of a philosopher, and the fire of a warrior. In a world divided by language, race, and ideology, Bruce Lee became a bridge—teaching us that greatness isn't found in choosing sides, but in transcending boundaries.

His journey wasn't just about becoming a martial artist. It was about becoming fully himself. And in doing so, he gave the world permission to do the same.

1.1 Early Life in Hong Kong and America

Bruce Lee wasn't born with a silver spoon or a grand destiny written on the walls of his childhood home. He was born Lee Jun-fan in San Francisco in 1940—during a performance tour of his opera-singer father. But shortly after, his family returned to Hong Kong, where his real journey began, amid the backdrop of a city scarred by war and occupied by poverty.

As a child actor, Bruce appeared in over 20 films by the time he was 18. His charm and screen presence were undeniable, but life off-camera was more turbulent. He got into fights, clashed with local gangs, and lived with a restlessness many young people feel—the ache of not knowing who they truly are.

To discipline his body and defend himself, he turned to Wing Chun, training under the legendary Ip Man. But martial arts did more than protect him—it started to shape his mind. He began to see that movement was expression, that form could lead to freedom.

At 18, Bruce was sent back to America—not as a star, but as a boy seeking purpose. He landed in Seattle with $100 in his pocket, working at a restaurant and teaching martial arts in parks and backyards. For most, this would be the story of hardship. For Bruce, it was the crucible of transformation.

In the melting pot of the U.S., Bruce Lee confronted racism, rejection, and ridicule. He was told he couldn't teach non-Chinese students. He was mocked for his accent. He was warned that "kung fu" would never make it in Hollywood. And yet, he persisted.

This part of Bruce's life holds a powerful truth for anyone striving for growth:

Where you start doesn't define you. How you respond does.

Every insult was fuel. Every barrier, a forge. Every challenge, a chance to train—his body, his mind, his spirit.

Self-Reflections: Your Answer Please:

- *What early struggle in your life became the ground for your growth?*

- *Are you using your pain as fuel or as an excuse?*

1.2 Lessons in Cultural Fluidity

Bruce Lee was not just a martial artist or movie star—he was a bridge between worlds.

Born in America. Raised in Hong Kong. Trained in Chinese martial traditions. Educated in Western philosophy. He danced between cultures like water, refusing to be boxed in by nationality, ethnicity, or identity.

When Bruce returned to the United States, he realized something profound:

Being caught between two cultures is not a curse. It's a gift—if you know how to use it.

At a time when Asian actors were typecast as villains, servants, or silent background characters, Bruce imagined something radical: an Asian hero with depth, strength, and humanity. He spoke fluent English with confidence, not apology. He taught kung fu to non-Chinese students at a time when it was taboo. He married Linda, a white woman, in an era when interracial marriage was still controversial in many parts of America.

He lived what few dared to live:

A life not limited by borders or traditions, but enriched by them.

Bruce Lee took the elegance of Chinese philosophy and the boldness of American individualism, blending them into a new way of being. His martial art, Jeet Kune Do, was not a "style" but a philosophy of openness—a fluid way of fighting that was rooted in principles, not rigid techniques.

This cultural fluidity wasn't easy. He was rejected by Hollywood executives, told that "an Asian lead wouldn't be believable" for

American audiences. He was criticized by traditional martial arts communities for being too unorthodox. But Bruce saw clearly:

Clinging to culture without evolution is not tradition—it's stagnation.

His lesson to us is timeless:

- Don't let your origin become your limitation.

- Your identity is not a cage—it's a canvas.

- True growth happens when you blend your roots with your reach.

Self-Reflections: Your Answer Please:

- *Where have you felt "in between" two worlds in your life—cultures, careers, beliefs?*

- *How can you turn that tension into a source of creativity and growth?*

2. The Artist in the Fighter

To the world, Bruce Lee was a fighter—fast, fierce, and fearless. But beneath the flying kicks and sharp jabs was something far deeper: an artist at heart.

Bruce didn't fight to destroy. He fought to express.

Every punch he threw had rhythm.

Every move had grace.

Every stance was like a brushstroke on the canvas of combat.

He didn't see martial arts as just technique or sport. For him, it was a living, breathing art form—a way to *paint* his emotions without using words. He spoke through movement, and every fight was a poem of power and presence.

He once told a student,

"Kick me. But not like an exhibit. Do it with emotional content— no anger, just expression."

This is what set Bruce apart. He wasn't imitating a style. He was *creating from the inside out.* Jeet Kune Do—his personal martial philosophy—wasn't a style at all. It was style-less. Formless. It was the art of removing what is unnecessary and keeping only what is true.

Life Lesson for Students:

In whatever you do—studies, art, career, coding, design, writing, leading—don't just repeat what's taught. Make it your own. Add your soul into it. Let it reflect *who you are*. That's where your real strength lies.

Bruce taught us that the most powerful warrior is not the one who copies 1,000 techniques… but the one who expresses 1 truth with everything he's got.

Be a fighter with soul. Be an artist in action.

2.1 His Love for Philosophy, Acting, and Martial Arts

"All types of knowledge ultimately mean self-knowledge." – Bruce Lee

Bruce Lee wasn't just fighting with fists—he was fighting with thought.

He wasn't just acting on screen—he was expressing a truth.

And he wasn't just practicing martial arts—he was searching for meaning.

Most people knew Bruce for his lightning-fast kicks and commanding screen presence. But behind the physicality was a mind as sharp and agile as his movements. Bruce was a voracious reader, consuming everything from Eastern mysticism and Western philosophy to psychology, poetry, and fitness science. His personal library held over 2,500 books, filled with annotations and reflections in the margins.

Philosophy wasn't separate from martial arts for Bruce—it was the core of it.

He saw every punch as a metaphor, every movement as a meditation.

From Krishnamurti to Nietzsche, from Taoism to Zen, Bruce was always exploring the big questions:

Who am I?

What is truth?

What does it mean to live freely?

And yet, Bruce didn't retreat into ivory towers. He brought philosophy to life—on the streets, in the dojo, on the movie set.

Acting was another expression of this deep quest. To Bruce, acting wasn't pretending—it was being. He once said, *"To express oneself honestly, not lying to oneself, that, my friend, is very hard to do."* This was his mission: to express his authentic self without compromise.

Whether through a fight scene or a single line of dialogue, Bruce's performances burned with realness. Every movie role became a stage for deeper truths. Every interview, a class in awareness.

In Bruce's world, martial arts were not for hurting people.

Acting was not for fame.

Philosophy was not for showing off intelligence.

They were all doors to the same room: self-realization.

His unique blend of mind, body, and soul made him unlike anyone before or after. He showed the world that a philosopher can have a six-pack, and a fighter can be deeply poetic.

Self-Reflections: Your Answer Please:

- *What are the three passions in your life that make you feel most alive?*

- *How can you use them together to express who you really are?*

2.2 Integrating Art and Self-Expression into Life

"Art calls for complete mastery of techniques, developed by reflection within the soul." – Bruce Lee

To Bruce Lee, life itself was art.

Not just something to live—but something to shape, mold, express, and evolve.

He believed that every person is an artist—not just painters, dancers, or actors—but anyone who dares to live authentically.

Bruce didn't separate art from life. He blurred the lines. For him, martial arts were not just combat—they were a form of self-expression. Acting wasn't just about performing—it was about revealing inner truth. His very movement, his speech, even his silence carried an artistic presence.

"The function and duty of a quality human being is the sincere and honest development of one's potential." – Bruce Lee

Bruce taught that self-expression is the highest form of growth. It is not about impressing others. It is about connecting with your deepest self and letting that truth shape your actions, your words, your choices—your life.

He didn't teach martial arts to create copies of himself. He encouraged students to find their own voice, their own style. This was the soul of his philosophy:

"Always be yourself. Express yourself. Have faith in yourself."

This integration of art and life shows us something vital:

- You don't need to be on a movie screen to live expressively.

- You don't need to throw a perfect sidekick to be graceful.

- You don't need to follow a script to be a performer.

Every decision, every day, every interaction is a blank canvas.

Bruce's legacy reminds us to create boldly, live honestly, and move with intention.

Living is not just about survival. It's about creation.

And the most important thing you'll ever create... is yourself.

Self-Reflections: Your Answer Please:

- *What parts of your life feel like art? What parts feel mechanical?*

- *How can you bring more of your true self into your daily life?*

- *Where are you copying others? Where are you expressing your unique voice?*

3. A LIFE OF FIRE: TRIUMPHS AND TRAGEDIES

Bruce Lee didn't just live—he burned.

His life was a flame—bright, intense, and all too brief. But in that short span, he shook the world with his passion, precision, and presence.

From the streets of Hong Kong to the studios of Hollywood, Bruce faced battles that weren't just physical—they were cultural, emotional, and deeply personal.

Triumphs:

- He broke racial stereotypes in a time when Asian actors were sidelined or caricatured.

- He revolutionized martial arts cinema—not just through action, but through *philosophy*.

- He created Jeet Kune Do, a philosophy of combat and life that inspired millions across generations.

- He proved that *one man with a vision* could shake an entire system.

But behind the spotlight, the warrior faced storms.

Tragedies:

- He struggled with being misunderstood—not just by critics, but by his own peers.

- Hollywood rejected his ideas initially, preferring safer, whiter faces for leading roles.

- He endured physical injuries, deep stress, and relentless pressure to "prove himself."

- His life was cut short at just 32—leaving behind a legacy that was still unfolding.

And yet, he never stopped burning.

"The key to immortality is first living a life worth remembering."

— Bruce Lee

Life Lesson for Students:

Bruce's story is a reminder that greatness is forged in fire. You will face doubts, rejections, and pain. But don't let them dim your light. Keep showing up. Keep expressing. Keep moving.

Even when the world resists you, *be too powerful to ignore*.

3.1 Injuries, Discrimination, and Setbacks

"Do not pray for an easy life, pray for the strength to endure a difficult one." – Bruce Lee

For all his confidence, charisma, and mastery, Bruce Lee's journey was not smooth.

It was filled with pain. With rejection. With moments that could've broken any ordinary man.

But Bruce was not ordinary.

The Injury That Nearly Ended Everything

In 1970, at the peak of his physical strength, Bruce suffered a devastating back injury while performing a routine warm-up—a herniated sacral nerve.

Doctors told him he might never walk again, let alone kick or perform martial arts.

For someone whose entire life revolved around movement, it was more than a physical blow—it was an identity crisis.

But Bruce didn't collapse.

Instead, he transformed pain into power.

While bedridden for months, he didn't wallow—he wrote. He read. He revised his philosophy.

Much of what became the core of *Jeet Kune Do* was born not in the dojo, but in his recovery bed.

He learned that the body can be injured, but the spirit must stay fluid and strong.

Facing Discrimination and Being "Too Chinese"

In Hollywood, Bruce faced another kind of injury—one to his identity.

He was told:

- "You're too Asian to be a leading man."

- "Americans won't relate to someone who looks like you."

- "We'll cast a white man to play the Kung Fu master instead."

He was even denied the lead role in a show he conceived, because he didn't "fit" the mold.

Imagine having the talent, the vision, the drive—and still being rejected for being yourself.

But instead of shrinking, Bruce created his own opportunities. He went back to Hong Kong, where he became a superstar overnight with *The Big Boss*, *Fist of Fury*, and *Way of the Dragon*. His success there forced Hollywood to look again.

He didn't wait for permission. He proved his worth through persistence.

The Universal Lesson of Setbacks

Bruce's injuries and setbacks weren't detours. They were tests. And they became his greatest teachers.

He showed us that:

- Pain is not the end—it is a portal to growth.

- Discrimination is not a wall—it is a mirror showing you what you must overcome.

- Setbacks are not signs to stop—they are signals to deepen your purpose.

Self-Reflections: Your Answer Please:

- *What injury—physical or emotional—has shaped you the most?*

- *Have you ever been judged or rejected for being "different"? What did it teach you?*

- *What setback in your life is actually preparing you for something greater?*

3.2 Resilience and Reinvention

"To hell with circumstances; I create opportunities." – Bruce Lee

There are people who endure.

And then, there are those who transform—who use their struggles not just to survive, but to reinvent themselves, again and again. Bruce Lee was one of them.

When most people think of Bruce, they imagine the fierce fighter, the action star, the global icon. But beneath all of that was a man who refused to be stuck—in labels, in roles, in the limits life tried to put on him.

From Actor to Philosopher to Fighter to Filmmaker

Bruce was a child actor in Hong Kong cinema. He could've stayed in that comfort zone.

But he chose a different path. He left the screen to study philosophy and martial arts in America. He worked as a dishwasher. A teacher. A thinker. A man constantly evolving.

When Hollywood shut him out, he didn't complain.

He didn't beg for roles.

He created his own movies. Directed his own fight scenes. Wrote his own scripts.

When an injury threatened to take away his ability to walk, he didn't stop training—he rewired his training, rewrote his philosophy, and emerged stronger.

Bruce didn't just recover. He reinvented.

- From student to teacher.

- From rejected actor to international superstar.

- From martial artist to philosopher in motion.

His life reminds us:

You are not fixed. You are fluid.

You are not what happens to you. You are what you do next.

The Power of Resilience

Bruce's form of resilience was not about brute endurance.

It was a kind of inner elasticity—the ability to bend, to adapt, to bounce back with wisdom and fire.

He believed in embracing the obstacle—not avoiding it. He saw setbacks as sparring partners, not enemies. And most of all, he trusted in his ability to create again—even from nothing.

"Empty your cup so that it may be filled; become devoid to gain totality."

This is the mindset of true reinvention—the courage to unlearn, relearn, and show up anew.

Self-Reflections: Your Answer Please:

- *Where in your life are you being called to reinvent yourself?*

- *What part of your identity do you need to let go of to grow further?*

- *Are you enduring life, or evolving through it?*

PART II:

THE CORE LESSONS – BRUCE LEE'S PHILOSOPHY FOR GROWTH

4. BE LIKE WATER

"Empty your mind.
Be formless, shapeless—like water.
You put water into a cup, it becomes the cup.
You put water into a bottle, it becomes the bottle.
You put it in a teapot, it becomes the teapot.
Now, water can flow... or it can crash.
Be water, my friend."

— Bruce Lee

This is perhaps Bruce Lee's most iconic teaching—and the most timeless.

Water is the perfect metaphor for life.

It's soft, yet it wears down stone.

It's humble—it always seeks the lowest place.

But it's also powerful enough to carve through mountains.

To Bruce, water symbolized the ideal way to live and fight:

- Without rigidity

- Without ego

- With awareness and adaptability

Water doesn't resist—it *responds*.

It doesn't fear change—it *becomes* change.

Life Lesson for Students:

In today's ever-changing world, being like water isn't just wise—it's necessary.

- When life throws unexpected situations, flow around them.

- When challenges rise, don't panic—adapt.

- When your plans don't go your way, reshape yourself, not your spirit.

- In learning, relationships, careers—stop clinging to fixed forms. Be fluid. Be free.

Water doesn't try to impress.

It just *is*.

And in just being, it transforms everything it touches.

Bruce didn't just say this. He lived it. Whether in acting, martial arts, or philosophy, he moved like water—shifting between cultures, breaking rules, and creating a space no one else dared to.

Want to be unstoppable? Don't try to control everything.

Instead, learn to move with life—like water.

4.1 Adaptability and Fluid Thinking

"Be water, my friend." - This isn't just Bruce Lee's most famous quote—it's a life philosophy, a blueprint for how to think, move, and grow.

Water has no fixed form, yet it shapes mountains.

It flows softly, yet it can crash with force.

It adapts, it adjusts, it persists.

Bruce Lee didn't just teach martial arts—he taught mental martial arts.

He challenged us to stop clinging to rigid patterns, and instead, learn how to flow.

What Is Fluid Thinking?

Fluid thinking means:

- Being open instead of attached to one idea.

- Adjusting your approach when the situation changes.

- Letting go of ego, and learning from everything—even your enemy.

- Knowing that strength is not in resistance, but in response.

Bruce created *Jeet Kune Do* as the embodiment of adaptability.

It wasn't a fixed style—it was "the style of no style." He refused to be bound by tradition or technique. He would absorb what worked from any discipline—boxing, fencing, wing chun, judo—and discard what didn't.

This was not rebellion. It was evolution.

"Use only that which works, and take it from any place you can find it."

Why Adaptability Matters in Life

We live in an age of rapid change. New jobs, shifting economies, evolving relationships, unexpected challenges.

Rigid thinkers break under pressure.

Fluid thinkers bend, re-align, and move forward stronger.

Bruce didn't just talk about this—he lived it:

- When movies rejected him, he turned to TV.

- When the U.S. market failed him, he pivoted to Hong Kong.

- When traditional martial arts confined him, he created his own path.

He trusted his inner compass more than the world's rules. And that made him unstoppable.

Self-Reflections: Your Answer Please:

- *Where in your life are you holding on too tightly?*

- *What would it look like to "be like water" in that area?*

- *What beliefs or routines do you need to let go of to adapt and thrive?*

Bruce Lee's life teaches us:

You don't need to be unbreakable—you need to be unstoppable.

And that comes from your ability to think, feel, and move... like water.

4.2 Stories from Real Fights and Acting Choices

"I fear not the man who has practiced 10,000 kicks once, but I fear the man who has practiced one kick 10,000 times." – Bruce Lee

Behind the movies, behind the speed and power, was a man who fought real battles—in the dojo, on film sets, and within his own mind.

The Wong Jack Man Fight – Philosophy in Action

One of the most legendary real-life fights in Bruce Lee's story was with Wong Jack Man, a traditional martial artist from San Francisco. The reason?

Bruce was teaching martial arts to non-Chinese students, breaking with tradition. Some elders didn't like it.

They challenged him to a fight.

The result? Bruce won in a matter of minutes. But he wasn't satisfied.

He felt the fight had taken too long. That his movements weren't efficient enough. That tradition had slowed him down.

This was a turning point. Bruce began dismantling rigid techniques and created Jeet Kune Do—his way of intercepting and responding freely, with no wasted motion.

It wasn't just about defeating someone. It was about evolving.

His Acting: Precision Meets Purpose

Bruce Lee's acting wasn't about showing off—it was about communicating energy, clarity, and truth.

Every movement, every glare, every pause on screen was *intentional*.

One of the best examples of this is the mirror scene in "Enter the Dragon."

In that final showdown, Bruce faces his opponent in a room of mirrors.

Instead of reacting with confusion, Bruce slows down, breathes, and breaks the mirrors—symbolically breaking illusion, ego, and deception.

That wasn't just a fight scene.

It was spiritual metaphor, woven into action.

He used cinema as a canvas for his beliefs:

- In "The Way of the Dragon," he fights Chuck Norris in the Colosseum—not with anger, but with *respect*. That fight is clean, powerful, and even sacred.

- In "Enter the Dragon," he brings Eastern philosophy to Western audiences—balancing fight choreography with moral clarity.

- In "Game of Death," his unfinished masterpiece, Bruce climbs through levels of enemies—each representing a different philosophy or skillset. He defeats them not with brute force, but with adaptability and awareness.

More Than Action – A Message in Every Move

Bruce Lee didn't act to be a star.

He fought to make movies more human, more real, and more truthful.

"The highest art is no art. The highest form is no form."

He blurred the lines between acting and reality, between fight and flow. And in doing so, he elevated martial arts from combat to conscious communication.

Self-Reflections: Your Answer Please:

- *Where in your life can you bring more intention to your actions—like Bruce on screen?*

- *What battles are you fighting that are calling you to evolve, not just win?*

- *Are you acting out of ego, or out of clarity and purpose?*

My Personal Story: Flowing Through Uncertainty

There was a time in my career when everything felt uncertain. The business I had poured my heart into had to be scrapped, not by choice, but by force of circumstances. I felt stuck, frustrated, and ready to fight the system. But then, I remembered Bruce Lee's words:

"Be formless, shapeless, like water."

Instead of resisting, I took a step back and adapted. I realigned my focus, found new ways to contribute, and eventually, that shift led me to a better opportunity. That experience taught me: control is an illusion; flow is power.

5. Hack Away at the Unessential

"It is not daily increase but daily decrease. Hack away at the unessential."

— Bruce Lee

In a world obsessed with *more*—more information, more goals, more pressure—Bruce Lee taught the opposite:

Success is not about adding. It's about subtracting.

He believed in stripping things down to their core truth. Whether it was in martial arts, philosophy, or life, he asked one powerful question:

"Is this truly necessary?"

Bruce's personal martial art, *Jeet Kune Do*, wasn't a collection of flashy moves. It was the removal of waste—no extra steps, no showmanship, just *pure effectiveness*.

That's how he lived too.

- He cut out limiting beliefs.

- He avoided meaningless talk.

- He focused only on what *mattered*—growth, truth, and expression.

Life Lesson for Students:

You don't need to *do more*.

You need to do less—better.

- Instead of studying 10 hours with distractions, study 3 hours with full focus.

- Instead of chasing every opportunity, go deep on the one that aligns with your values.

- Instead of pleasing everyone, learn to *listen to yourself*.

Greatness is not found in clutter. It's found in *clarity*.

"Simplicity is the key to brilliance." — Bruce Lee

Let go of what no longer serves you.

Cut the noise. Clear the mental desk.

And in that space, let your true self shine.

5.1 Minimalism in Thought, Training, and Life

Bruce Lee didn't just move with speed—he moved with clarity.

He didn't believe in clutter—not in his fighting, not in his thinking, and not in his way of life.

To him, simplicity was the highest level of mastery.

He believed the more we strip away, the more we uncover our true power.

Minimalism in Thought: Clarity Over Complexity

Bruce immersed himself in deep philosophical texts—Taoism, Buddhism, Krishnamurti.

But he didn't let complexity confuse him. He always brought it back to something clear, sharp, and practical.

He would ask:

- *"Does this idea help me live better?"*

- *"Does this belief make me freer or more fearful?"*

He believed that wisdom isn't about knowing more—it's about seeing clearly.

This is why his quotes are so short, yet so deep. He wasn't trying to impress—he was trying to liberate.

Minimalism in Training: Efficiency Over Excess

Bruce practiced martial arts obsessively—but he didn't do a hundred techniques. He mastered a few, deeply.

He cut out what was ornamental. He removed anything flashy that didn't serve the fight.

His method, *Jeet Kune Do*, was built on this principle:

No fixed form. Only what works.

No wasted movement. Just flow, function, and freedom.

He would test everything—if a move took too long or too much energy, it was gone.

His workouts were simple, but intense.

His routines were focused, not fancy.

His goal was maximum impact with minimum effort.

Minimalism in Life: Living with Purpose, Not Pressure

Bruce wasn't interested in status. He wore simple clothes, trained in garages, read in silence.

He didn't seek attention—attention came to him because of his authenticity.

He taught that the more we let go of things—possessions, ego, distractions—the more we become ourselves.

He practiced:

- Saying "no" to roles that didn't align.

- Letting go of friendships that didn't uplift.

- Refusing to live someone else's version of success.

"Empty your cup so that it may be filled."

This wasn't just a Zen saying—it was how he lived every day.

Self-Reflections: Your Answer Please:

- *What are the "unessential" things in your mind, habits, or schedule that you need to hack away?*

- *Where in your life are you overcomplicating what should be simple?*

- *What would your life look like if you lived by "less, but better"?*

Minimalism wasn't a trend for Bruce—it was a path to truth.

He showed us that clarity, not clutter, is where true strength begins.

5.2 Decluttering Your Inner and Outer World

Bruce Lee was a master of cutting through the noise—internally and externally.

He understood something many people never realize:

The path to greatness is not about adding more. It's about letting go.

Letting go of:

- Mental chatter

- Emotional baggage

- Useless techniques

- False identities

- Unnecessary possessions

Decluttering the Inner World

Bruce spent hours each day in quiet reflection. Not to escape—but to return to center.

He studied philosophy, wrote personal reflections, and often questioned his own thoughts.

He once said:

"The mind is like a fertile garden—it will grow anything you plant: flowers or weeds."

His goal?

To weed out the doubts, fears, and limiting beliefs that didn't serve him.

To remove the clutter of comparison, pride, and expectation.

To leave behind a clear mind—ready to respond, not react.

This is why he loved stillness. He used silence as a weapon.

He trusted in deep self-awareness, not shallow confidence.

Decluttering the Outer World

Bruce didn't surround himself with excess.

- His training equipment? Simple and homemade.

- His wardrobe? Basic and comfortable.

- His environment? Clean, functional, focused.

He believed your surroundings reflect your state of mind.

A cluttered room? A cluttered focus.

A noisy life? A distracted soul.

That's why he created space—not just in his home, but in his lifestyle.

He chose:

- Fewer commitments, deeper presence.

- Fewer techniques, sharper results.

- Fewer possessions, more purpose.

Decluttering as a Way to Realign with Your Essence

Bruce wasn't chasing freedom.

He was removing what blocked it.

Just like a sculptor removes stone to reveal the statue, Bruce removed noise to reveal his authentic self.

Every "no" he said was a "yes" to clarity.

Every distraction he cut was a gift to his purpose.

Self-Reflections: Your Answer Please:

- *What beliefs, thoughts, or stories are cluttering your inner peace?*

- *What activities, commitments, or things in your environment feel heavy or draining?*

- *What can you let go of this week to move closer to clarity and power?*

Decluttering is not about emptiness—it's about creating space for meaning.

Bruce Lee's life reminds us: You don't need more to become more. You need less of what blocks you from being who you truly are.

My Story: Letting Go to Grow

Early in my coaching journey, I believed I had to offer everything—career tips, leadership tools, personal development, technical know-how—all at once. I thought more was better. But it only overwhelmed people... and me.

Then I remembered Bruce Lee's insight:

"It's not the daily increase but the daily decrease. Hack away at the unessential."

I sat down, took a hard look at my work, and removed the fluff. I focused only on what truly transformed lives. That clarity created space—for my work to deepen and my impact to grow.

6. Express Your Authentic Self

"Always be yourself. Express yourself. Have faith in yourself."

— Bruce Lee

To Bruce Lee, the ultimate purpose of martial arts—and life—was self-expression.

He wasn't interested in becoming the next master of an ancient tradition. He wanted to break tradition if it didn't serve truth. He wanted to move, speak, and live from a place that was *real*—not rehearsed.

He once said:

"The individual is more important than any established style or system."

That's why he created Jeet Kune Do—not as a style to follow, but as a *path to create*.

A living philosophy that changed as he changed.

He believed that every human being has a unique voice, rhythm, and energy. The only real failure is to *deny yourself* and try to become someone else.

Don't be a copy.

Don't mold yourself for others' expectations.

Instead—burn off everything that's false and let your real self emerge.

Life Lesson for Students:

The world doesn't need another version of someone else.

It needs you—raw, real, and relentless.

- Speak your truth, even if it trembles.

- Create from your heart, not for applause.

- Stand out by standing in your values.

- Your authenticity is your *superpower*.

Bruce's power didn't come from being perfect.

It came from being fully himself—flaws, fire, and all.

And in doing that, he gave the world something no one else could offer.

"Showing off is the fool's idea of glory."

Real glory? It's simply being you, all in.

6.1 The Journey from Imitation to Innovation

Every great creator starts by copying.

Bruce Lee was no exception.

He studied the greats. He mirrored his masters. He learned the rules.

But what made him *legendary* was that he didn't stop there.

He transformed imitation into innovation.

And in doing so, he transformed himself—and the world around him.

Imitation: The Foundation of Mastery

Bruce began his martial journey in Wing Chun, under the legendary Ip Man.

He was a hungry student—curious, precise, respectful of tradition.

He also absorbed from fencing, boxing, judo, wrestling, philosophy—imitating the essence of excellence wherever he found it.

He even mimicked fighters' moves in movies, copying punches and kicks frame-by-frame.

But Bruce was never satisfied with just being "as good as." He was always asking:

"How can this be better? How can this be *mine*?"

Breaking the Mold: Rebellion with Purpose

As Bruce evolved, he began to see the limits in rigid systems.

- He felt trapped by styles that wouldn't allow creativity.

- He questioned rituals that lacked real-world application.

- He challenged hierarchies that rewarded obedience over truth.

His boldest move?

He rejected all fixed styles, including the very ones that raised him.

This wasn't arrogance. It was evolution.

He wasn't disrespecting tradition—he was transcending it.

"If you always put limits on everything you do, it will spread into your work and your life."

Innovation: Creating from the Core

Bruce Lee created Jeet Kune Do—not as a style, but as an *expression* of freedom.

It wasn't about learning more. It was about learning what to let go of.

He innovated by:

- Combining what worked from multiple disciplines.

- Discarding rituals that didn't serve the moment.

- Trusting his inner intelligence over external approval.

His innovation came from deep self-trust, endless experimentation, and the courage to be misunderstood.

He didn't just fight differently. He thought differently.

He didn't just act on screen. He redefined what it meant to be Asian in Hollywood—bringing pride, strength, and elegance to every role.

From Copying to Creating: Your Journey

Bruce's path is the universal creative journey:

1. Learn the rules.

2. Master the techniques.

3. Question the structure.

4. Break what limits you.

5.   Build what frees you.

You may start by following someone else—but you're meant to become yourself.

Self-Reflections: Your Answer Please:

- *In what areas of life are you still imitating, instead of innovating?*

- *What parts of your path need to be questioned—or broken— to find your own flow?*

- *What unique combination of skills, insights, and experiences are ready to become something new through you?*

Bruce Lee's legacy is not about perfection—it's about personal evolution.

He didn't just master a craft. He created a new way to move, think, and live.

From imitation to innovation—this is the path of greatness.

6.2 Building Your Unique Identity

Bruce Lee didn't just master martial arts—he mastered himself.

He wasn't trying to fit in.

He wasn't trying to be the next *someone else*.

He was fiercely focused on becoming the first and only Bruce Lee.

And that's the ultimate journey:

From following others... to *forging yourself*.

Identity Is Not Given. It's Created.

Bruce was born in San Francisco, raised in Hong Kong, and returned to America as an outsider.

He was too Western for the East, too Eastern for the West.

A Chinese man in a white man's world. A martial artist in a movie industry that saw Asians as sidekicks or stereotypes.

He had every reason to conform—to water down who he was to fit in.

But instead, he leaned in. He carved out his own space. He said:

"I'm not in this world to live up to your expectations, and you're not in this world to live up to mine."

That mindset wasn't just rebellious—it was liberating.

The Tools He Used to Shape His Identity

    1. Radical Self-Inquiry

Bruce constantly asked: *Who am I, really?*

He journaled deeply. He observed his thoughts. He questioned his habits.

2. Creative Fusion

He combined East and West, discipline and freedom, strength and grace.

His identity wasn't one thing—it was a fluid integration of everything that mattered to him.

3. Selective Rebellion

He didn't rebel for attention—he rebelled with intention.

When tradition limited him, he broke it.

When culture boxed him in, he stepped out.

4. Living Authentically in Every Role

Whether he was training, acting, or teaching, Bruce didn't "perform."

He embodied his truth—every gesture, word, and decision reflected who he really was.

Your Identity is Your Weapon

Bruce Lee taught us that your greatest power isn't your technique, talent, or title.

It's your authenticity.

The courage to:

- Stand in your values when it's uncomfortable.

- Speak your truth, even when it shakes things up.

- Create something new instead of copying what already exists.

When you live from your truth, you stop trying to fit the mold—and start *becoming the model*.

Bruce's Identity Lessons, Applied to Your Life

- *You're not your job, your status, or your past.*

- *You're a work of art in progress.*

- *You are not meant to "find" yourself—you're meant to build yourself, intentionally.*

Bruce didn't wait for permission.

He didn't follow the map.

He became the map.

Self-Reflections: Your Answer Please:

- *What aspects of your identity have been shaped by others' expectations?*

- *What qualities, passions, or values feel most true to you— even if they don't fit your environment?*

- *If you stopped trying to be accepted, who would you start becoming?*

Bruce Lee didn't try to "be someone."

He became himself so fully that the world couldn't ignore him.

That is the power of building a unique identity—one clear, courageous choice at a time.

My Story: Breaking the Mold

For many years, I played it safe. I spoke the language others wanted to hear. I worked hard but hid parts of myself—my deeper beliefs, my vision, my fire. When I started coaching engineers and professionals, I hesitated to share my spiritual side or my personal philosophy.

But Bruce Lee reminded me:

"Always be yourself, express yourself, have faith in yourself."

I took that leap. I began speaking from my truth—not from what I thought would impress. That's when real transformation began, both in me and those I worked with.

7. Discipline Over Motivation

"The successful warrior is the average man, with laser-like focus."

— Bruce Lee

Motivation is fleeting. It's a spark—a burst of energy that can ignite passion for a moment. But discipline is the flame that keeps burning, even when motivation fades.

Bruce Lee understood this better than anyone. He knew that greatness doesn't come from feeling inspired every day. It comes from having the discipline to show up when the excitement has worn off. The discipline to keep improving, no matter the challenges. The discipline to follow through on the vision—even when no one else believes in it.

Whether it was perfecting his kick or learning to move between cultures, Bruce didn't rely on temporary bursts of enthusiasm. Instead, he built a life based on habit—daily actions that aligned with his long-term vision.

Motivation will come and go.

But discipline? That's what carries you when the motivation is long gone.

Life Lesson for Students:

Discipline is what makes the difference between dreams and reality. It's what separates the occasional achiever from the unstoppable force.

- Don't wait for the perfect moment—create it with your discipline.

- Don't rely on fleeting inspiration—show up, even when you don't feel like it.

- Practice daily, and the results will speak for themselves.

Bruce Lee didn't just practice for the applause. He practiced because he was committed to mastery, not just in martial arts—but in life itself.

Discipline is the bridge between goals and accomplishment.

You don't need motivation to succeed.

You just need discipline. Every day. Every step.

7.1 Daily Training and Commitment

"Long-term consistency trumps short-term intensity." – Bruce Lee

Bruce Lee was not just a master of moments—he was a master of daily discipline.

Behind the speed, strength, and charisma was something quieter… but far more powerful:

A commitment to train, improve, and evolve—every single day.

His greatness wasn't a sudden explosion.

It was the compounding result of small actions done with devotion.

Bruce's Training Was His Temple

He didn't treat training like a chore.

He treated it like a spiritual practice—a place to sharpen his body, mind, and will.

A typical day in Bruce's life might include:

- 2–3 hours of martial arts drills

- Strength training and isometric workouts

- Shadowboxing and heavy bag work

- Stretching and mobility

- Reading philosophy and journaling

- Teaching students and reviewing film

- Meditating and refining new moves

And he still made time for family, writing, and film work.

"If you love life, don't waste time. For time is what life is made of."

He *didn't have more time* than others—he just used it more deliberately.

Consistency > Complexity

Bruce didn't believe in overloading his day with 100 activities.

He believed in refining the essentials—over and over again.

- One punch, done right, 1,000 times.

- One concept, applied in many ways.

- One idea, lived fully.

He trained when tired.

He trained when rejected by film studios.

He trained while recovering from injuries.

Because commitment is not about how you feel—it's about what you've decided.

Training Was More Than Physical

Yes, Bruce built an elite physique.

But more importantly, he trained his mind and spirit every day.

He journaled about fear, ego, and clarity.

He read Lao Tzu, Krishnamurti, Alan Watts.

He practiced silence, observation, and deep self-awareness.

To Bruce, *being strong* meant:

- Being mentally flexible

- Emotionally grounded

- Spiritually awake

Your Daily Practice = Your Future Identity

Bruce's daily routine wasn't random.

It was the ritual that aligned him with who he wanted to become.

He knew:

"What you do daily, you become permanently."

You don't become focused—you train it.

You don't become disciplined—you show up.

You don't become free—you earn it, one consistent day at a time.

Self-Reflections: Your Answer Please:

- *What daily actions are shaping you into the person you don't want to be?*

- *If your current habits continued for 5 years, who would you become?*

- *What is one small, consistent practice you can begin today to align with your highest self?*

Bruce Lee wasn't addicted to motivation.

He was committed to momentum.

Discipline didn't restrict him—it liberated him.

Through training, he didn't just build a body—he built a mind that could move mountains.

7.2 Mastery Through Consistent Effort

Mastery is not for the talented.

It's for the relentlessly consistent.

Bruce Lee was not born a master.

He became one—through daily, deliberate, focused effort.

His greatness wasn't an act of genius.

It was the result of refining the fundamentals with obsessive care.

Repetition with Intention

Bruce understood that doing something over and over is not enough.

The key is: doing it better each time.

He called this *"refining your instrument."*

Whether it was a punch, a scene, or a speech—he worked it again and again... until it wasn't just good. It was real.

He didn't chase variety.

He chased depth.

The Mindset of a Master

Bruce never saw mastery as a final goal.

To him, it was a state of being.

- A master is someone who can see simplicity in complexity.

- Who is more interested in growth than recognition.

- Who shows up when no one is watching—and gives 100%.

"Knowledge will give you power, but character gives you respect."

Bruce focused on building inner mastery:

Discipline. Humility. Patience. Precision.

Because outer strength fades—but *inner alignment lasts*.

Small Efforts, Compounded Over Time

Bruce's life was proof of the compounding power of:

- One more push-up.

- One more hour of study.

- One more scene rehearsed.

- One more failure, reflected upon.

He didn't seek *big wins*.

He committed to *small efforts*, done daily, without drama.

That's how he became a legend—not because of how fast he rose, but how deeply he rooted.

Flow Over Force

Mastery isn't about force.

It's about flow—a natural expression of who you are becoming.

Bruce aligned his actions with nature, movement, and presence.

He wasn't grinding—he was growing.

He flowed like water.

And over time, water shapes mountains.

Self-Reflections: Your Answer Please:

- *What's one small skill or habit you can commit to mastering through daily repetition?*

- *Where are you expecting results without putting in consistent effort?*

- *What would your life look like if you chose mastery over multitasking?*

Mastery is not a finish line.

It's a devotion to progress, regardless of speed or applause.

Bruce Lee didn't wait for perfect conditions.

He created transformation through small acts, done with fierce presence.

So can you.

My Story: The Power of Daily Repetitions

Building a new habit—whether it's meditation, writing, or physical training—is never about a lightning bolt of inspiration. I've failed countless times by waiting to "feel ready."

But Bruce's words kept echoing in my mind:

"I fear not the man who has practiced 10,000 kicks once, but the man who has practiced one kick 10,000 times."

So I stopped chasing motivation and started showing up. Every day. Even for just 12 minutes. That discipline became the heartbeat of my personal growth.

This idea mirrors the concept in my own book, Automate Your Growth, where I introduce a simple yet powerful practice: 12 minutes a day. A small commitment — yet over time, it compounds into massive growth.

Like Bruce Lee's "10,000 kicks," my 12-minutes daily habit become the space where repetition meets transformation.

8. Fearless Living

"Do not fear failure. Fear is the enemy. Fear is the greatest obstacle to growth. There is no fear in the mind of a warrior."

— Bruce Lee

Bruce Lee lived by a profound truth: Fear is the barrier between where you are and where you could be.

Fear isn't just about physical danger. It's the fear of failure, rejection, judgment, and even success. Fear keeps us small, stagnant, and stuck. It convinces us that we're not enough, that we should stay safe, or that we'll never make it.

Bruce refused to live in fear.

He didn't fear failure—because he knew failure was just a step on the path to success.

He didn't fear the unknown—because he saw the unknown as an opportunity to grow.

He didn't fear the opinions of others—because he knew the only opinion that mattered was his own.

"A warrior does not give up what he loves, he finds the love in what he does." — Bruce Lee

Life Lesson for Students:

Fear is an illusion. It paralyzes you, limits you, and distorts your reality. To live fearlessly is to embrace life as it comes—with courage, clarity, and a willingness to face discomfort head-on.

- Fear of failure? Fail fast, fail forward.

- Fear of judgment? Own your uniqueness.

- Fear of the unknown? Dive in. Explore.

Bruce didn't wait for the perfect moment to act. He didn't sit back and wait for his fears to subside. He took action despite them, and in doing so, he showed us that living fearlessly is the key to becoming unstoppable.

The only thing you need to fear is fear itself.

The true warrior's strength is not in avoiding fear, but in facing it with full presence, confidence, and courage.

8.1 Courage in Confrontation and Career

Courage isn't just about facing an enemy in a fight.

It's about standing your ground when your truth is on the line.

It's about speaking up, showing up, and rising up—even when the odds are against you.

Bruce Lee lived this courage—in every confrontation, and every career move.

Confrontation in Combat

Bruce wasn't just a performer—he was a real fighter.

And he didn't run from confrontation.

He faced it. With clarity. With calm. With complete conviction.

Real Fight Stories:

- In Oakland, he was challenged by the martial arts establishment for teaching Chinese martial arts to non-Chinese students.

- Instead of backing down, he faced the challenge head-on.

- He won—but realized he needed to be *faster, stronger, freer*—which led him to reimagine his entire fighting philosophy.

- In the streets of Hong Kong and the gyms of America, Bruce's name echoed not just because he could fight—but because he refused to back down from injustice, arrogance, or tradition when it blocked truth.

For Bruce, a fight wasn't just physical—it was an opportunity to prove character.

Confrontation in Career

Bruce's greatest battles weren't fought in a ring.

They were fought in Hollywood boardrooms and cultural backdrops.

- He was told his accent was too thick.

- That Asians couldn't be leading men.

- That America "wasn't ready" for his kind of charisma.

But Bruce didn't shrink to fit their version of success.

He expanded his own vision until the world had no choice but to look his way.

When Hollywood said no, he returned to Hong Kong—and made his own movies.

When they ignored his talent, he became too powerful to ignore.

The Source of Bruce's Courage

Bruce's courage came from:

- A deep belief in his mission

- Relentless inner clarity

- Years of training his body and mind under pressure

He wasn't fearless.

He had simply trained himself to act despite fear.

"Do not pray for an easy life, pray for the strength to endure a difficult one."

Your Courage, Unlocked

Courage isn't just for crisis. It's for:

- Speaking up in a meeting

- Saying no to a toxic job

- Creating your own path

- Choosing your purpose over popularity

Bruce's life reminds us:

You don't wait to feel brave.

You act bravely—and let courage catch up.

Self-Reflections: Your Answer Please:

- *Where are you shrinking your voice to avoid confrontation?*

- *What fear in your career is asking for a courageous decision?*

- *If Bruce were in your shoes today, what bold step would he take?*

Courage isn't loud.

It's stillness in chaos.

It's the refusal to compromise your truth.

It's the ability to look doubt, rejection, and fear in the eye—and keep walking.

Bruce Lee didn't just teach martial arts.

He lived the martial spirit—with courage in every confrontation, and conviction in every career move.

So can you.

8.2. How to Confront Your Inner Limitations

The greatest opponent you'll ever face isn't outside.

It's within.

Doubt. Fear. Ego. Insecurity.

These are the invisible forces that quietly shape—or shatter—your potential.

Bruce Lee didn't just conquer others.

He confronted his inner self—daily.

His true mastery began the moment he realized: "It is not the daily increase but daily decrease. Hack away at the unessential."

Bruce vs. Bruce

Bruce wrestled with:

- Fear of failure in Hollywood

- A near-paralyzing back injury

- Being rejected because of race

- The pressure to be a perfect fighter, teacher, and actor

- The weight of being a pioneer with no role model to follow

But he didn't deny these things.

He didn't run from them.

He faced them head-on—with radical honesty.

He journaled. He meditated. He reflected deeply.

Because he knew:

The limitations you don't confront become the prison you live in.

His Process of Inner Confrontation

1. Observe Without Judgment

    He trained himself to watch his emotions and thoughts like clouds passing by.

    No suppression. No attachment. Just awareness.

2. Question Every Belief

    He often asked, *"Why do I believe this? Where did it come from?"*

    Many of our limitations are inherited, not chosen.

3. Challenge With Action

    Every fear was met with practice.

    Every insecurity was met with repetition.

    He didn't wait for confidence—he *earned* it through effort.

4. Detach From the Ego

    Bruce said:

"Empty your cup so that it may be filled."

He knew ego was the mask that hid growth. So he dropped it—again and again.

Your Inner Fight: Where Growth Begins

Ask Yourself :

- *What story am I telling myself that keeps me small?*

- *Where am I blaming circumstances instead of taking ownership?*

- *What truth about myself am I afraid to face?*

These questions aren't comfortable.

But they're essential.

Bruce faced himself daily—not to shame or punish—but to liberate.

Self-Reflections: Your Answer Please:

- What emotion or belief do I avoid confronting the most? Why?

- Where in my life do I feel "stuck," and what internal fear is behind it?

- What would change if I saw my inner limitations not as flaws, but as doorways to freedom?

Insight

Bruce taught us:

You cannot defeat what you don't acknowledge.

You cannot grow until you let go.

To confront your inner limitations is to meet your true power.

Not by fighting yourself—but by facing yourself with courage, clarity, and compassion.

That's the path of a true warrior.

And it's open to anyone willing to take that first, honest step.

My Story: Speaking When My Voice Trembled

One of the most terrifying decisions I made was to step away from the secure government job and then business path and follow my mission to empower engineers. I questioned myself: "What if I fail? What if people don't understand this vision?"

But Bruce's words came through like a call to battle:

"Do not pray for an easy life. Pray for the strength to endure a difficult one."

I realized fear would always exist. But it didn't have to lead. That decision—to move forward *with* fear—was the turning point. Because true fearlessness isn't the absence of fear, it's the courage to act anyway.

9. THE WARRIOR MINDSET

The warrior mindset is not just about physical strength or fighting techniques. It's about how you approach life, challenges, and your own growth. Bruce Lee was a master of transforming his mind, sharpening it like a blade, and using it to break through the barriers of life.

A true warrior doesn't just fight battles—they choose them wisely.

A true warrior doesn't just react—they respond with clarity.

A true warrior doesn't just endure—they thrive under pressure.

Bruce Lee's warrior mindset was built on four core principles:

1. Mental Discipline

   Bruce understood that mental strength is just as important as physical ability. He trained his mind with as much dedication as he did his body. The warrior mindset requires relentless focus and the ability to control your thoughts, emotions, and reactions.

   o   Clarity over chaos—train your mind to stay clear, even in the most stressful situations.

o   Decisiveness over doubt—make choices with confidence, even when the path isn't clear.

2. Emotional Resilience

A warrior doesn't let emotions rule their actions—they use them. Bruce didn't repress his emotions, but he understood how to channel them into focused energy. Whether facing criticism, injury, or personal struggles, he never allowed external circumstances to control his inner peace.

o   Acceptance over resistance—embrace challenges as part of your growth.

o   Control over chaos—manage emotional responses, rather than being controlled by them.

3. Adaptability and Flexibility

Bruce Lee's martial philosophy wasn't about rigid forms or following rules blindly. It was about adapting to the situation, the opponent, and the environment. Flexibility in the mind and body allows you to flow with life's challenges, rather than break against them.

o   Fluidity over force—be like water: adaptable and responsive, not rigid and reactive.

o   Innovation over imitation—find your unique approach, and adapt it to each circumstance.

4. Unyielding Focus

Warriors are known for their ability to stay focused on the goal, even in the face of distractions and obstacles. Bruce Lee's unwavering focus on his purpose—whether it was becoming a martial arts master, breaking down cultural barriers, or evolving his philosophy—was the foundation of his success.

o   Purpose over distractions—stay true to your vision and your mission, even when the world tries to pull you off course.

o   Commitment over comfort—dedicate yourself to your goals, no matter how difficult the path may seem.

Life Lesson for Students:

The warrior mindset isn't about being fearless, invincible, or perfect. It's about having the strength to keep moving forward, the resilience to face challenges, and the wisdom to grow from every battle you encounter.

- Be intentional with your thoughts and actions.

- Embrace failure as part of the process.

- Adapt to changing circumstances.

- Stay focused on your true purpose.

9.1 The Balance of Calm and Power

To the outside world, Bruce Lee was speed, power, and explosive energy.

But those who knew him... saw something deeper: stillness.

Not laziness.

Not passivity.

But a centered presence that gave his power direction and purpose.

Calm is not the absence of strength.

Calm is the control of it.

Power Without Calm is Chaos

Bruce trained hard. He hit fast. He kicked with precision.

But he also breathed deeply, observed silently, and moved with intention.

He wasn't just a fighter—he was a philosopher in motion.

He knew:

- A restless mind leads to wasted motion.

- A reactive spirit loses power in emotion.

- Only a calm heart can fully express strength.

"A quick temper will make a fool of you soon enough."

His Secret Weapon: Emotional Mastery

Bruce had the ability to:

- Stay calm in public conflict

- Stay present during rejection and judgment

- Stay grounded while rising to global fame

He didn't let emotion hijack performance.

He didn't let praise inflate his ego.

He didn't let anger poison his focus.

This wasn't natural—it was trained.

Just like he trained his punches... he trained his peace.

Stillness Was Part of His Practice

Bruce meditated.

He reflected deeply in journals.

He walked in silence.

He sat in stillness.

Because he knew:

True clarity only comes when the mind is quiet.

He wasn't trying to escape the world.

He was trying to master his response to it.

Power That Waits Is Stronger Than Power That Reacts

When you have calm, you gain:

- Control over your words

- Precision in your decisions

- Deep access to your intuition

You stop reacting to everything.

You start responding with wisdom.

"It is not a daily increase, but a daily decrease. Hack away at the unessential."

That's calm.

That's power.

Self-Reflections: Your Answer Please:

- *Where in my life am I mistaking noise for strength?*

- *What situations consistently steal my calm—and why?*

- *How can I practice stillness, even for 2 minutes a day, starting now?*

Bruce didn't just explode with power—he chose when and how to release it.

He didn't just shine under pressure—he thrived in it because of his calm.

In a world that rewards speed and reaction,

Bruce reminds us:

Stillness is strength. Calm is courage. Quiet is clarity.

Let your power come from presence

9.2 Dealing with Failure, Criticism, and Chaos

"In the middle of chaos lies opportunity." – Bruce Lee

What separates a master from the rest?

It's not that they don't fail.

It's that they know how to fall and rise again—cleaner, sharper, wiser.

Bruce Lee didn't escape failure.

He embraced it, learned from it, and used it as fuel.

He faced rejection, racism, injury, and misunderstanding—but never let it define him.

Failure as Feedback, Not Finality

Bruce's journey was not smooth:

- His *first major TV project*, The Green Hornet, got canceled after one season.

- Hollywood executives repeatedly turned him down for lead roles because he was Asian.

- He suffered a serious spinal injury in 1970 and was told he might never kick again.

But each setback became a pivot point, not a dead end.

Instead of asking, *"Why me?"*

He asked, *"What's next?"*

"Defeat is a state of mind; no one is ever defeated until defeat has been accepted as a reality."

Criticism Was His Companion

Bruce was criticized for:

- Being too intense

- Breaking martial arts tradition

- Teaching "secrets" to non-Chinese students

- Mixing philosophy with fighting

- "Acting" like a movie star when he was "just" a fighter

But he didn't shrink to please anyone.

He stayed rooted in his truth.

"I'm not in this world to live up to your expectations and you're not in this world to live up to mine."

Chaos as Creative Fuel

Bruce didn't just survive chaos—he *transformed* it.

When Hollywood shut the door, he didn't complain—he went back to Hong Kong and made his own films.

When his body broke, he used stillness to heal and sharpen his mind.

When life spun out of control, he returned to simplicity and clarity.

He flowed like water—not by avoiding chaos, but by moving through it with grace and intent.

Lessons from Bruce on Chaos

1. Control Your Response, Not the World

    You can't control critics, failures, or sudden changes.

    But you can master your reaction.

2. Turn Pain into Presence

    He used physical pain, emotional setbacks, and societal rejection as fuel to go deeper into his craft and self-awareness.

3. Simplify Under Stress

    When chaos strikes, the answer isn't to do more. It's to do less, better.

    That was Bruce's approach.

Self-Reflections: Your Answer Please:

- *What failure have I not yet redefined as feedback?*

- *Whose criticism am I giving too much power to?*

- *How can I turn my current chaos into an opportunity for clarity or reinvention?*

Bruce showed us that you don't overcome failure and criticism by being invincible.

You overcome by being authentic, adaptable, and aligned with your purpose.

"Absorb what is useful, discard what is not, add what is uniquely your own."

That's how you deal with chaos:

Not with control—but with creativity and character

My Story: Strength in Silence

There was a point in my life when I was misunderstood, even criticized by people I deeply respected. My instinct was to explain, defend, or retaliate. But then I remembered how Bruce faced criticism—not with noise, but with poise.

"A wise man can learn more from a foolish question than a fool can learn from a wise answer."

I chose silence. Not weakness, but still strength. That space allowed me to grow past ego and into peace.

PART III:

THE APPLICATION – BRUCE LEE'S WISDOM FOR MODERN LIFE

10. Mind Like Water: Mindfulness and Focus

Bruce Lee often spoke of the mind as being like water—fluid, adaptable, and clear. Just as water adjusts to its container, the mind must be able to flow with whatever life presents. But to do this, it must first be clear and focused.

The mind of a warrior, like water, is free from clutter, distraction, and negativity. It is fully present in the moment and ready to respond—*not react*—to the ever-changing circumstances around it.

Bruce Lee practiced mindfulness in his everyday life. His focus was not just on achieving great things in martial arts or acting—it was about cultivating the ability to fully immerse himself in whatever he was doing, with complete presence.

Mindfulness in Action:

1. Clarity Over Distraction

   In a world full of distractions—social media, expectations, external noise—Bruce Lee's wisdom reminds us that clarity is our most powerful asset. When the mind is clear, decisions become simpler, actions more effective, and life more purposeful.

- o Discipline over distraction—train your mind to stay focused on your goals, no matter how much the world tries to pull you in different directions.

- o Being present over being busy—when you focus, you don't have to rush. Everything will unfold in due time.

2. Non-Attachment to Outcome

Water doesn't cling to anything. Similarly, the mind of a warrior is not attached to the results—it is focused on the process, the action, and the learning. When you stop obsessing over outcomes and trust the journey, your performance improves, and stress fades away.

- o Let go of fear—trust in your preparation, and detach from the pressure of "winning" or "losing."

- o Focus on the process—mastering the art of being fully immersed in what you're doing, without concern for the future.

3. Flow State and Adaptability

Like water flowing effortlessly, a focused mind adapts to whatever comes its way. Bruce Lee's philosophy on fighting—of flowing with the opponent's movements, responding rather than reacting—can be applied to everyday life.

o   Adaptability over rigidity—flow with the challenges, adapt your response, and don't hold onto a fixed way of thinking.

o   Effortlessness over struggle—when you're in the zone, there's no struggle, only natural, fluid action.

4. Calm Under Pressure

A true warrior, like water, remains calm under pressure. The mind does not panic when faced with obstacles; it assesses, adjusts, and reacts with clarity. Bruce Lee taught that the mind, when trained in mindfulness and focus, can face any challenge with poise.

o   Calmness over chaos—train your mind to remain calm, even in intense situations.

o   Clarity in chaos—when you practice mindfulness, you can see through the noise and focus on the right actions.

Life Lesson for Students:

True mastery begins in the mind.

When you cultivate a mind that is clear, focused, and present, you unlock your true potential—not only in martial arts but in every area of life. In school, work, relationships, and personal growth, mindfulness and focus are what separate the successful from the stressed.

- Clear your mind of unnecessary thoughts—like Bruce, focus only on what truly matters to you.

- Immerse yourself in the present moment—fully experience what you're doing without distractions or regrets.

- Face each challenge with the mindset of a warrior—calm, clear, and ready for action.

10.1 Presence in Action

Presence is not just a spiritual concept.

It's a *skill*. A *discipline*. A *practice*.

Bruce Lee didn't just move.

He moved with such intensity, clarity, and aliveness, you couldn't take your eyes off him.

Whether he was fighting, acting, or speaking—he was fully present.

He wasn't just in the moment.

He *was* the moment.

The Flow State of a Master

In every fight scene, every kick, every line of dialogue—Bruce operated in flow.

No hesitation. No second-guessing. Just pure, undivided attention.

How?

He trained his mind and body to become *one*.

No split between thought and action.

Just clear intent and clean execution.

"When the opponent expands, I contract. When he contracts, I expand. And when there is an opportunity... I do not hit. *It hits all by itself.*"

That's presence in action.

What Presence Looks Like in Daily Life

- In a conversation: fully listening, not waiting to reply

- In your work: one task, total attention, no noise

- In a workout: feeling every breath, every movement

- In a crisis: responding, not reacting

Presence turns ordinary actions into extraordinary performances.

It turns effort into *art*.

And time into *timelessness*.

Bruce's Training in Presence

1. Breath Awareness – Centering his energy through deep, conscious breathing

2. Single-Minded Practice – Repeating moves until the *thinking* disappeared

3. Body as Expression – Every action was a reflection of his emotional and mental state

4. Journaling + Reflection – Sharpening his awareness beyond the physical

Flow Like Water: Responsive, Not Reactive

Bruce's core idea—"Be like water"—wasn't just about flexibility.

It was about presence without resistance.

- Water doesn't hesitate.

- It doesn't plan.

- It flows, adapts, and fills the shape of the moment.

You don't have to control everything when you're *present enough to move with it.*

Self-Reflections: Your Answer Please:

- *What situations do I rush through without true presence?*

- *Where in my life do I need to shift from reaction to response?*

- *What daily activity can I turn into a mindfulness practice starting today—just like Bruce did with movement?*

Insights:

Presence in action isn't about perfection.

It's about being fully alive in what you're doing—whether you're giving a speech or washing dishes.

Bruce Lee's legacy isn't just in what he did.

It's in *how he did it*—with full presence, raw truth, and deep focus.

You don't need to be a martial artist to move like him.

You just need to show up, fully, to this moment.

Because this moment is where your power lives.

10.2 Meditation and the Martial Artist's Mind

Why Bruce Meditated

Most people know Bruce Lee as a fighter.

Fewer know he was a seeker—deeply reflective, emotionally aware, and spiritually awake.

He meditated not to escape the fight, but to enter it more completely—with clarity, calm, and control.

To Bruce, the mind of a martial artist had to be:

- Empty yet aware

- Still yet responsive

- Detached yet alert

Meditation was the tool that helped him live that balance.

"Meditation is the discovery that the point of life is always arrived at in the immediate moment." — a quote Bruce resonated with deeply from Alan Watts

What He Practiced Mentally

1. Mindfulness of Breath

   Focusing on his breath to anchor awareness—especially before fights or filming.

2. Visualization

   Seeing success in his mind before it happened.

   He'd rehearse scenes, moves, and even outcomes mentally—then let go.

3. Emptiness Training

   Letting go of thoughts, identity, and fear to enter "no-mindedness" (*mushin* in Japanese).

   This allowed instinct to take over.

4. Philosophical Meditation

   He reflected on Taoism, Zen, and Jiddu Krishnamurti's teachings, contemplating the nature of self and reality.

Meditation as a Martial Tool

In martial arts, milliseconds matter.

The one who hesitates, who overthinks, who tenses—loses.

Meditation helped Bruce:

- Slow down time internally

- Detach from fear and ego

- React without thought—pure response

- Train his nervous system to stay relaxed under pressure

"The consciousness of self is the greatest hindrance to the proper execution of all physical action." – Bruce Lee

Stillness = Superpower

Bruce didn't need a mountain cave or incense.

His meditation happened:

- While walking

- While training

- While sitting silently in his backyard

- Even while writing his personal journals

Presence was his temple.

Stillness was his gym.

Awareness was his real weapon.

Self-Reflections: Your Answer Please:

- *What does stillness mean to me? Have I experienced it?*

- *How can I use my breath to anchor myself when I'm overwhelmed?*

- *What fear or thought often clouds my performance—and how can I observe it without judgment?*

Insight:

Bruce Lee showed us that meditation isn't reserved for monks or mystics.

It's for fighters. Leaders. Creators. Humans.

You don't meditate to become someone else.

You meditate to become fully you—awake, aware, aligned.

"Empty your mind. Be formless, shapeless—like water."

In that emptiness, your true power begins.

My Story: Stillness Before the Storm

Before major events—webinars, live talks, or deep coaching sessions—I used to feel jittery. Thoughts raced. "Will this go well? Will people get value?"

Then I started practicing presence, just like Bruce trained his mind before entering the ring. I began each session with 60 seconds of stillness.

"Don't think. Feel."

That shift changed everything. My mind settled. I connected deeper. And people could feel that calm. Bruce taught me that mental clarity is more powerful than any script.

11. Move with Purpose: Career and Goals

"A goal is not always meant to be reached, it often serves simply as something to aim at."

— Bruce Lee

Bruce Lee's philosophy about life, including career and goals, was always centered around purpose. He didn't just want to be a successful martial artist or actor—he wanted to change the world, break cultural boundaries, and create something lasting. His every move had a purpose—and this is the mindset we can adopt for our own careers and goals.

In the world of modern distractions and constant change, it's easy to get lost in the hustle. But just like Bruce Lee's approach to martial arts, success in your career and personal goals requires clarity, discipline, and an unwavering sense of purpose.

Key Principles for Moving with Purpose:

1. Know Your 'Why'

    Bruce Lee didn't just fight for fame or recognition. He fought for the deeper purpose of martial arts—to share his art, to break through cultural stereotypes, and to express himself authentically. Every action he took was aligned with his core values and his why.

- o Define your purpose—understand why you do what you do. Is it to help others? To create something meaningful? To express your true self?

- o Connect your work to your values—when you understand your "why," your work becomes more than just a task—it becomes your mission.

2. Set Intentional Goals

Goals are like the compass guiding you on your journey. They are the target, but not the end. Bruce Lee taught us that goals are important not just for achievement, but for direction. Every decision he made in his career was aligned with his overarching purpose of creating something meaningful and authentic.

- o Set clear, purposeful goals—define what success looks like for you, but also ensure those goals are aligned with your deeper values.

    ○ Measure growth, not just results—sometimes the process of reaching a goal is more important than the goal itself.

3. Commit to Consistent Action

Bruce Lee didn't just talk about his dreams—he acted on them, every day. His dedication to his craft was unwavering. Whether he was training his body or studying philosophy, he committed to constant improvement, regardless of how small the steps seemed. The key to moving with purpose is not in big bursts of energy, but in consistent action toward your goals.

    ○ Take small, deliberate steps every day toward your career goals. It's not about doing it all at once, but about staying on course.

    ○ Embrace discipline over motivation—you don't need to feel "inspired" to take action. When you move with purpose, even the smallest actions matter.

4. Adapt Your Approach

As Bruce Lee showed us, adaptability is key. Just as water molds itself to fit any container, your approach to achieving your goals should be flexible enough to evolve with circumstances. The world is constantly changing, and being rigid or stuck in one way of thinking can limit your growth. Adapt, learn, and improve with each experience.

- o Stay flexible—don't get stuck in one way of doing things. Be open to change and adapt your strategies when necessary.

- o Learn from every experience—whether you succeed or fail, there's always a lesson. Each step is part of your growth.

5. Seek Balance

Bruce Lee's philosophy was about finding balance in life. He believed in integrating the mind, body, and spirit. Success in your career and personal life doesn't come from single-minded obsession. It comes from creating a life where each element—work, health, relationships, and growth—works in harmony.

- o Balance work and life—your career should support your well-being, not drain it. Make time for physical activity, mental relaxation, and emotional nourishment.

o   Stay grounded in your values—balance doesn't mean splitting your focus, but aligning every aspect of your life with your core beliefs.

Life Lesson for Students:

To move with purpose is to have a clear direction and to take intentional action toward that goal. Just as Bruce Lee focused his energy on his passion for martial arts, you too can channel your time and efforts toward creating a career that is meaningful and fulfilling.

- Define your mission—don't just work for a paycheck.

- Set meaningful goals that align with your values.

- Consistently move forward, step by step, with determination.

- Be adaptable and willing to change course when necessary.

- Seek balance to sustain long-term success.

11.1 Pursuing Excellence, Not Fame

Bruce Lee became a global icon.

But that was never his intention.

He didn't chase cameras.

He chased truth.

He didn't seek applause.

He sought alignment with his inner standard.

Fame was a result.

Excellence was the mission.

Why Bruce Refused to Be a "Star"

Bruce often clashed with Hollywood. Why?

Because they wanted him to be a stereotype.

A sidekick. A silent warrior. A symbol.

But Bruce didn't fit in anyone's mold.

He didn't want to "be seen." He wanted to express something real.

"I'm not trying to be the next anyone. I'm trying to be the first Bruce Lee."

Excellence Is Internal

To Bruce, success wasn't measured by:

- Box office numbers

- TV ratings

- Social popularity

It was measured by:

- Precision in a kick

- Clarity of a thought

- Authenticity in action

- Living aligned with his truth

He didn't ask, *"Will this make me famous?"*

He asked, *"Is this my best?"*

What It Takes to Pursue Excellence

Bruce trained with obsessive intent.

Not to beat others—but to surpass himself.

He wrote:

"I fear not the man who has practiced 10,000 kicks once, but the man who has practiced one kick 10,000 times."

Excellence is boring.

Repetitive. Demanding.

But it leads to true mastery—and that was Bruce's currency.

Fame Is Loud. Excellence Is Quiet.

Fame comes from outside.

It's about recognition, trends, followers.

Excellence begins inside.

It's about craft, discipline, honesty.

Bruce once said:

"To hell with circumstances; I create opportunities."

That's the voice of someone focused on *what he can control*—not how the world perceives him.

Self-Reflections: Your Answer Please:

- *Am I chasing attention or alignment?*

- *Where have I compromised excellence to fit in, be liked, or be seen?*

- *What would I still do every day—even if nobody noticed?*

Insight:

Bruce Lee didn't become a legend by trying to be legendary.

He just tried to be authentic, awake, and excellent—every single day.

Fame may fade.

But character echoes.

So don't ask how to get more attention.

Ask: *What is worth giving my full, focused energy to?*

Pursue excellence—and let the world catch up when it's ready

11.2 Defining Success on Your Terms

Success According to Bruce Lee

Bruce didn't live to *impress the world*.

He lived to *express the truth*.

While others chased trophies, status, or money, Bruce asked:

"Is what I'm doing aligned with who I am becoming?"

To him, success wasn't about beating others.

It was about becoming more of who you truly are.

How the World Defines Success (and Why Bruce Rejected It)

The world's version:

- Big income

- Big following

- Big titles

- Constant comparison

- External validation

Bruce's version:

- Inner clarity

- Physical, mental, and emotional mastery

- Creative expression

- Alignment of thought, speech, and action

- Peace in motion

He didn't reject success—he redefined it.

Build Your Own Definition:

Bruce believed in crafting a life from the inside out.

He asked us to examine what *we* truly value.

"If you love life, don't waste time, for time is what life is made of."

Success, then, becomes:

- Doing meaningful work

- Staying true under pressure

- Growing a little every day

- Creating something that reflects your essence

How to Start Living by Your Terms

1. Define Your Values

   What principles guide your decisions when no one's watching?

2. Detach from Comparison

   Bruce didn't want to be the next anyone.

   He wanted to be unrepeatable.

3. Measure Growth, Not Just Goals

   Did you learn today? Did you act with courage? Did you train your body or mind?

4. Let Integrity Be Your Success Metric

   Are your actions in alignment with your inner voice?

Self-Reflections: Your Answer Please:

- *What has "success" meant to me—and where did that definition come from?*

- *What does success feel like—not just look like—for me?*

- *If I removed fear and comparison, what kind of success would I pursue?*

Bruce Lee didn't just teach us to punch faster or think deeper.

He taught us that real power comes from being true to yourself—and building success around *that truth*.

"A goal is not always meant to be reached, it often serves simply as something to aim at."

You don't need permission to define your own path.

You just need presence, courage, and self-faith.

That's real success.

My Story: Defining My Success

There was a phase when I chased numbers—more followers, more income, more visibility. But it felt hollow. I asked myself, "What am I really doing this for?"

Bruce's life reminded me that he didn't act for fame—he acted with purpose. Every move, every film, every philosophy came from his inner compass.

"A goal is not always meant to be reached. It often serves simply as something to aim at."

I redefined success: living in alignment with my calling and helping others grow freely. Since then, everything I do flows from that purpose.

12. Train Every Day: Habits and Rituals

"The more we value things, the less we value ourselves."

— ***Bruce Lee***

For Bruce Lee, mastery wasn't a one-time event—it was a daily commitment. Every day, he worked on sharpening his mind, body, and spirit. His habits and rituals were not just about physical training—they were about creating a lifestyle that aligned with his deeper purpose.

In our fast-paced world, it's easy to get distracted by immediate gratification or external pressures. But, as Bruce Lee demonstrated, true success is the result of consistent effort over time.

Key Principles for Daily Training:

1. Mastery Through Consistency

    Bruce Lee didn't rely on bursts of inspiration. His success was built on habit—small, consistent actions taken every day, with dedication and intention. Whether he was training his body, refining his technique, or expanding his knowledge, Bruce understood that mastery comes through daily practice.

- o Consistency over intensity—don't worry about doing everything perfectly. Just show up every day and do your best.

- o Small improvements every day—don't expect instant results. Focus on improving by 1% every day, and over time, those small improvements add up to massive success.

2. Developing Strong Rituals

Bruce Lee's life was full of rituals that kept him grounded and focused. These rituals weren't just physical practices; they were mental and emotional habits that helped him stay on track. Whether it was meditation, visualization, or physical training, these rituals helped him stay disciplined and aligned with his goals.

- o Create daily rituals that help you stay focused and balanced. This could include meditation, morning exercise, journaling, or even the 12-minute daily habit.

o   Prioritize your rituals—make time for your rituals every day, no matter how busy you are. These moments of calm and focus will center you.

3. Physical and Mental Training

Bruce Lee was known for his intense physical training, but he was equally committed to developing his mind. He read philosophy, practiced martial arts, and even developed his own unique approach to training. Both body and mind were essential to his philosophy of growth. True success requires developing both.

o   Train the body and the mind—don't neglect one for the other. Practice physical discipline through regular exercise, but also commit to mental training through learning, reading, and self-reflection.

o   Balance strength and flexibility—as Bruce Lee famously said, be like water: adaptable and fluid in mind and body.

4. Push Through Plateaus

Bruce Lee understood that growth is not linear. There are times when progress seems to stall, and the work feels repetitive. But he knew that success comes when you push through these plateaus. By consistently putting in the effort, even when results aren't immediately visible, you break through and reach new heights.

- o Embrace the plateau—don't get discouraged when progress feels slow. Stay consistent, and trust that growth is happening beneath the surface.

- o Challenge yourself daily—step outside of your comfort zone regularly. Keep raising the bar for yourself, and aim for continuous improvement.

5. Self-Reflection and Adaptation

Bruce Lee was also a master of self-reflection. He continually assessed his own progress and adapted his habits to improve further. The key to consistent growth is not just doing the same thing every day but constantly adapting and refining your approach based on your reflections.

- o Reflect on your progress—take time each day or week to assess what's working and what's not. Adjust your habits accordingly.

- o Be open to change—don't be afraid to change your approach if something isn't working. Growth comes from adapting and evolving.

Life Lesson for Students:

Success is the result of consistent habits and daily rituals. Bruce Lee didn't just train hard—he trained smart. His daily habits were the foundation of his greatness, and we can all learn from his commitment to constant self-improvement.

- Focus on progress, not perfection—every small action you take each day brings you closer to your goals.

- Create habits that align with your goals—be intentional about the rituals that shape your life and your future.

- Adapt and grow—stay flexible in your approach and always reflect on how you can improve.

12.1 The 10,000 Kicks Principle

The Myth of Variety vs. The Power of Depth

In a world that glorifies multitasking, variety, and novelty—Bruce stood for something else:

Repetition with intention.

Focus with intensity.

Depth over distraction.

Anyone can dabble.

But mastery requires devotion to the fundamentals.

Whether it's a side kick, a business habit, or a meditation practice—doing it *again and again*, with mindful attention, is where growth lives.

Why This Principle Matters

Repetition builds:

- Muscle memory – Your body learns faster than your mind.

- Confidence – When you've done something 10,000 times, doubt disappears.

- Clarity – Each rep reveals a new layer of insight.

- Resilience – You get comfortable with the boredom, discomfort, and grind of mastery.

Bruce turned repetition into art—and that's what made him unbeatable.

Beyond Martial Arts: Where This Principle Applies

- Public Speaking – Master one story, one speech, and refine it every time.

- Fitness – Perfect one movement (like a push-up or squat) to transform your body.

- Relationships – Practice one act of kindness daily—it will deepen your connection.

- Self-awareness – Observe one emotional pattern regularly, and it will dissolve.

Mastery is not in doing more, but in doing less, better.

The Formula Behind the Principle

Repetition × Awareness × Time = Mastery

But here's the twist:

- Repetition without awareness is burnout.

- Awareness without repetition is theory.

- Time without intensity is waste.

Bruce combined all three—he didn't just *repeat* kicks.

He studied them, challenged them, refined them.

Self-Reflections: Your Answer Please:

- *What is the "one kick" in my life I need to practice more deeply?*

- *Am I chasing novelty when I should be mastering the basics?*

- *Where can I commit to depth instead of dabbling?*

The 10,000 kicks principle teaches us this:

Repetition with presence leads to excellence.

Mastery is not a result of talent—but of tuned, relentless practice.

You don't need more things to do.

You need one thing done with 10,000 levels of depth.

That's how Bruce Lee became a legend—not by doing everything, but by doing one thing like no one else ever could.

12.2 Designing Your Daily Growth Practice

Bruce's Life as a Living Dojo

Bruce didn't separate life from training.

To him, every action—walking, writing, thinking, moving—was a chance to grow.

Growth wasn't something he scheduled.

It was something he lived.

His day included:

- Mind training (reading, writing, reflecting)
- Body training (martial arts, fitness, flexibility)

- Spirit training (philosophy, meditation, awareness)

He wasn't waiting for the perfect moment.

He created small, intentional rituals that added up to mastery.

How to Build Your Own Daily Growth Practice

You don't need 8 hours a day.

You need clarity, consistency, and commitment.

Here's how to start:

1. Morning Mindset Activation

"As you think, so shall you become."

- 5 minutes: Silence or breath awareness

- 3 minutes: Write 1 clear intention for the day

- 2 minutes: Visualize yourself acting with clarity, courage, or calm ,OR

- 12 minutes : Daily habit, from my book "Automate Your Growth"

What it does: Aligns your mind before the world distracts you.

2. Body as a Temple Ritual

"The body is an instrument of the mind."

- 15–30 minutes: Movement (martial arts, yoga, run, stretch)

- Focus on presence, not perfection

- Track progress with joy, not pressure

What it does: Anchors your awareness in motion—like Bruce.

3. The 10-Minute Learning Drill

- Read or listen to something inspiring or skill-building

- Write 1 idea you'll apply that day

- Teach or share it with someone briefly

What it does: Turns knowledge into wisdom through action.

4. Evening Reflection & Refinement

"Mistakes are always forgivable, if one has the courage to admit them."

- 5 minutes: What did I do well today?

- 3 minutes: Where did I fall short or act unconsciously?

- 2 minutes: What will I improve tomorrow?

What it does: Turns your day into feedback for growth—not judgment.

Customize with Bruce Lee's Values

Pick 1–2 of the following Bruce-inspired themes to rotate weekly:

- Simplicity – What can I remove today to make space for flow?

- Self-expression – Did I act authentically today?

- Adaptability – How did I flow like water today?

- Focus – What one kick did I practice today?

Self-Reflections: Your Answer Please:

- *What one practice brings me alive, and how can I honor it daily?*

- *Where am I wasting energy on distraction instead of depth?*

- *How can I turn ordinary moments into sacred practice?*

You don't grow by reading more quotes.

You grow by living one quote completely, every day.

Bruce Lee didn't wait to become great.

He trained, reflected, simplified, and *became*—day by day.

So should you.

My Story: My 12-Minute Practice

People often ask me how I manage growth with consistency. The truth? I train daily—but not for hours. Just 12 focused minutes.

That came from Bruce's philosophy—daily, intentional, simple practice.

"Long-term consistency trumps short-term intensity."

Whether it's reading, writing, reflection, or spiritual connection— those 12 minutes shape the rest of my day. Bruce taught me: greatness is not built in bursts. It's built in rhythm.

13. Live with Impact: Influence and Legacy

"To me, the extraordinary aspect of life is not in what we get from it, but in what we contribute to it."

— Bruce Lee

Bruce Lee didn't just want to be known as a martial artist or actor—he wanted to create an impact that lasted far beyond his lifetime. His influence stretched across cultures, inspiring generations to break free from limitations, embrace self-expression, and pursue mastery in their own lives. His legacy continues to shape the worlds of martial arts, film, and personal development, reminding us that true leaders don't just follow—they create their own path.

To live with impact is to not only achieve personal success but to inspire and uplift others, leaving behind a legacy that will live on long after you're gone.

Key Principles for Living with Impact:

1. Be True to Your Authentic Self

Bruce Lee's approach to martial arts was revolutionary because he created his own path, blending traditional martial arts with innovative techniques to form Jeet Kune Do. He never followed trends—he followed his own truth. His commitment to authenticity inspired millions to seek their own true selves, rather than imitate others.

○ Live by example—be authentic in everything you do. People are inspired by those who are true to themselves.

○ Break conventions—don't be afraid to challenge the status quo. Live by creating new ways to approach old problems.

2. Inspire Through Action

Bruce Lee didn't just talk about change—he embodied it. His life was a testament to the power of taking action toward your goals. His success wasn't based on his words alone, but on the consistent actions he took every day to improve himself and the world around him. True leaders inspire others through their actions, not their intentions.

○ Live your values—don't just speak about what you believe. Live it, and let your actions be the reflection of your vision.

o   Challenge the status quo—inspire others by leading with courage and pushing boundaries.

3. Create a Vision Bigger Than Yourself

Bruce Lee's vision was not just about his own fame or success—it was about creating a cultural shift, breaking racial barriers, and elevating martial arts to an art form. He sought to inspire others to think beyond their immediate goals and to create something that would outlast them. Leaders with impact think about legacy—what will they leave behind? What impact will they have on future generations?

o   Think beyond yourself—what impact do you want to leave on your industry, community, or the world?

o   Inspire others to lead—a true leader empowers others to create their own path and make their own impact.

4. Embrace Responsibility

Living with impact means taking responsibility for your actions, words, and influence. Bruce Lee understood that true mastery came with the responsibility of using his platform and influence to inspire positive change.

Leadership is not about control—it's about taking responsibility for the impact you make on others.

o Own your influence—whether positive or negative, recognize the impact your actions have on others.

o Live with integrity—make decisions based on what is right, not what is easy or convenient.

5. Leave a Legacy of Empowerment

Bruce Lee's greatest gift wasn't just in his martial arts skills; it was in his ability to empower others to break free from their limitations. His philosophy of self-expression and personal freedom continues to inspire millions. A true leader creates a legacy of empowerment—encouraging others to reach their full potential.

o Empower others to grow—help those around you discover their strengths and encourage them to take charge of their own growth.

o Create opportunities—offer platforms for others to shine, and share the spotlight to allow others to lead.

Life Lesson for Students:

Living with impact means inspiring others to create their own greatness, and leaving behind a legacy that continues to influence and empower future generations. Bruce Lee showed us that true leadership is about being authentic, consistent, and empowering others to step into their own power.

- Create a vision that extends beyond your own success.

- Live with integrity—be the example others want to follow.

- Empower others—your true legacy is in how you lift up those around you.

13.1 Leadership Through Character

Bruce Lee: A Reluctant but Powerful Leader

Bruce never asked to be followed.

He simply *lived with intensity, integrity, and purpose.* And people couldn't help but be drawn to him.

He led:

- With his presence, not his position.

- With his example, not his ego.

- With vision, not domination.

His leadership didn't come from power.

It came from character.

What Made Bruce a Leader?

1. Authenticity – He didn't try to be anyone else.

"Always be yourself, express yourself, have faith in yourself."

2. Discipline – He lived what he preached.

   He trained harder than anyone. He practiced what he taught.

3. Clarity – He knew who he was and what he stood for.

   He didn't let the world define him.

4. Compassion – Behind the fierce exterior was deep care for others.

   He mentored, taught, uplifted.

5. Fearlessness – He confronted discrimination, failure, injury—and rose stronger.

   His courage gave others courage.

Leadership Is Not About Followers

It's about:

- Leading yourself when no one's watching

- Making decisions rooted in values, not fear

- Speaking the truth even when it's uncomfortable

- Showing up consistently, even when it's hard

Bruce didn't "command" respect.

He earned it by being real, reliable, and relentless.

Character Traits Bruce Modeled (That You Can Practice)

Trait	Bruce's Example	Your Daily Application
Integrity	Spoke against Asian stereotypes	Speak your truth respectfully
Humility	Kept learning from others—even when famous	Stay a student, always
Grit	Trained relentlessly, even after injury	Keep going when it's hard
Focus	Practiced one kick 10,000 times	Simplify your goals and give them full attention
Compassion	Taught students from all races and backgrounds	Help others grow—without ego or need for praise

Self-Reflections: Your Answer Please:

- *Do I live in a way that others would want to follow—not because I tell them to, but because they feel inspired?*

- *What values define my leadership?*

- *Where do I need to lead myself more consistently before expecting to lead others?*

You don't need a stage or spotlight to lead.

You just need clarity, courage, and character.

Bruce led by being the message.

He didn't yell it. He lived it.

"Knowledge will give you power, but character gives you respect."

In a noisy world chasing attention—be someone who earns trust.

That's leadership through character.

That's *the Bruce Lee way*.

13.2 Building a Legacy Through Self-Mastery

Legacy is Not What You Leave Behind—It's What You Live Daily

Bruce never set out to be a legend.

He set out to be fully alive, fully real, and fully expressive.

His legacy wasn't carved in statues.

It was forged in his choices, his values, and his relentless growth.

That is how real legacies are made.

The Inner Journey That Built an Outer Impact

Bruce Lee was constantly mastering:

- His body (through discipline and training)

- His mind (through study, philosophy, and thought)

- His emotions (through awareness and calm in chaos)

- His spirit (through meditation and self-inquiry)

And that's the secret:

Self-mastery is the seed. Legacy is the fruit.

What Does Self-Mastery Look Like in Daily Life?

It's not perfection—it's progression.

Self-mastery is when:

- You choose growth over comfort

- You respond consciously instead of reacting impulsively

- You do what's right when no one's watching

- You practice your values, not just talk about them

Bruce didn't "try to be great."

He tried to be honest with himself—and in that honesty, he became legendary.

Steps to Begin Building Your Legacy—Today

1. Define Your Core Values

   What virtues do you want people to feel when they meet you?

   (e.g., clarity, compassion, courage, calm)

2. Commit to Daily Practice

   Legacy is not built in leaps—but in the consistency of character.

3. Simplify and Go Deep

   Find your "one kick" and give it 10,000 intentional repetitions.

4. Express Your True Self Boldly

   Don't die with your truth still inside.

Speak it. Share it. Live it.

5. Serve Others with What You've Mastered

    Bruce didn't keep his wisdom to himself.

    He taught, guided, and lifted others with it.

Self-Reflections: Your Answer Please:

- *If I lived today fully in alignment with my highest values, what would that look like?*

- *What part of myself needs more practice, not perfection?*

- *What will be my "one thing" that the world remembers— not because I said it, but because I lived it?*

Bruce Lee's legacy wasn't his fame.

It was his self-mastery—his devotion to being fully, freely, and fiercely himself.

And you are invited to do the same.

You don't need a stage or a spotlight to become unforgettable.

You just need to show up as your truest self, every day.

That's how you build a legacy—not by trying to be someone... but by becoming *yourself*, fully.

So start now.

Start small.

But start.

The world needs your truth.

Just like it needed Bruce's.

My Story: Coaching From the Heart

When I first began mentoring engineers, I focused on performance—getting them better jobs, more income, bigger promotions. But something felt incomplete. Bruce's legacy reminded me:

"To hell with circumstances; I create opportunities."

And even more deeply: *"The key to immortality is first living a life worth remembering."*

So I shifted. I began coaching from a deeper place—not just to help them succeed, but to help them feel alive, authentic, and impactful. That's the kind of leadership Bruce stood for—and the kind I now strive to embody.

14. The Tao of You: Crafting Your Growth Path

"To me, the greatest thing is not to be perfect, but to be truly oneself."

— Bruce Lee

Bruce Lee's philosophy was not just about physical strength or martial arts—it was about creating a life that was authentic, impactful, and constantly evolving. To Bruce Lee, life was a flowing process, a continuous journey of self-discovery and growth. This process, which he often referred to as the Tao, was the path of becoming—a constant state of growth and self-improvement.

The Tao of You is about crafting a personal path to growth, where you actively shape your journey, adapt along the way, and live in alignment with your true self. It is the culmination of the principles you've learned, brought together in a way that is unique to your life and your goals.

Key Principles for Crafting Your Growth Path:

1. Embrace Continuous Evolution

    Just as Bruce Lee transformed martial arts, he constantly evolved as a person. He didn't just stick with one style, one philosophy, or one way of thinking—he was open to change and adaptation. The Tao of You is not about reaching a final destination; it's about the continuous process of becoming.

- o Embrace change—don't fear evolution. Your growth path will never be linear; there will be twists, turns, and transformations. Welcome them.

- o Challenge old beliefs—growth often means shedding outdated ideas and embracing new ones that align with your true self.

2. Find Harmony Between Mind, Body, and Spirit

Bruce Lee's philosophy was deeply rooted in the idea of balance. True growth isn't just about physical strength or intellectual knowledge—it's about aligning the mind, body, and spirit. True mastery comes when all three aspects of your being are in harmony.

- o Integrate mind-body practices—physical training, mental focus, and spiritual practices such as mindfulness or meditation should be an ongoing part of your journey.

o Prioritize well-being—take care of your health and emotional well-being, recognizing that growth is not just external, but internal as well.

3. Craft a Path of Authenticity

Bruce Lee was not afraid to forge his own path. He encouraged others to express themselves authentically, not to follow the molds set by others. Your growth path must reflect your uniqueness, your talents, and your true desires.

o Create a life that reflects your values—make choices that align with who you are and what you want to create in the world.

o Be unapologetically yourself—don't try to fit into a mold. The world needs your unique contribution.

4. Be Present in Your Journey

The Tao of You is not about rushing to the end goal. It's about fully embracing each moment of the process. Bruce Lee was deeply invested in the present, whether he was training, teaching, or creating. Presence in the moment allows you to experience life more deeply and make more conscious choices.

- o Live in the moment—take time to appreciate the journey and recognize that growth happens as much in the process as it does in the destination.

- o Practice mindfulness—focus on your thoughts, actions, and emotions as they arise, without judgment.

5. Trust in the Process

Bruce Lee had an unshakable belief in the power of personal growth. He trusted that by working consistently and living in alignment with his principles, he would evolve into the best version of himself. Your path will be full of challenges, but by trusting in the process of growth, you can find peace and direction.

- o Trust yourself—believe in your ability to grow and adapt. Each step you take on your path is part of your evolution.

- o Embrace the journey—even when you face setbacks, remember that each experience is a stepping stone toward your ultimate growth.

6. Stay Open to Learning

Bruce Lee was always a student of life. Despite his incredible success, he never stopped learning and growing.

He took wisdom from a variety of sources, always seeking
to expand his knowledge. Your growth path should be a
lifelong journey of learning, where you constantly seek
new knowledge and experiences to broaden your horizons.

- o Seek wisdom from diverse sources—don't limit yourself
  to one approach. Learn from various traditions, books,
  mentors, and experiences.

- o Be curious and humble—recognize that you can always
  learn something new, no matter how much you've
  achieved.

Life Lesson for Students:

The Tao of You is the continuous, evolving journey of self-
discovery and growth. It's about crafting a path that aligns with
your values, where you embrace change, stay authentic, and trust
the process. By committing to growth every day, you create a life
full of meaning, purpose, and impact—just as Bruce Lee did.

- Create your unique path—don't follow the crowd. Your
  path is meant to be unique and authentic to you.

- Embrace change and growth—always be willing to evolve
  and adapt as you move forward.

- Trust the process—growth is a journey, not a destination.

14.1 Journaling Prompts, Exercises, and Actions

"To know oneself is to study oneself in action with another person." – *Bruce Lee*

This isn't the end of the book—it's the beginning of your real practice.

Use these prompts, exercises, and action plans to deepen your understanding of yourself, sharpen your character, and build your legacy—just like Bruce did, one moment at a time.

Self-Reflections: Your Answer Please:

Use these in your morning or evening journaling sessions:

Identity & Authenticity

- *Who am I without external roles, titles, or expectations?*

- *Where am I conforming, and how can I start expressing my true self more freely?*

Growth & Mastery

- *What's one thing I want to master in this life—and why?*

- *What's one small step I can take daily toward that mastery?*

Resilience & Courage

- *How did I respond to discomfort today? What did I learn from it?*

- *What fear is quietly running my decisions—and how can I face it directly?*

Presence & Awareness

- *What distracted me today? What centered me?*

- *How present was I in my body, breath, and emotions?*

Legacy & Leadership

- *What values do I want to be known for?*

- *If today were the last day of my life, did I live it aligned with those values?*

Bruce-Inspired Daily Exercises

1. The "One Kick" Challenge

Pick one action—physical, mental, or spiritual—and repeat it daily for 30 days.

Example: one movement, one affirmation, one deep breath before speaking.

2. Mirror Mindfulness

Stand in front of a mirror and ask:

- *Am I living with integrity today?*

- *What am I hiding from?*

Hold your gaze for one full minute in silence.

3. Flow Like Water Drill

Write about a situation that didn't go your way.

Ask: *How can I flow around this, adapt, and grow stronger—like water?*

4. The Simplicity Sweep

Every week, remove one thing (object, habit, thought) that clutters your life.

Ask: *Is this useful, beautiful, or true?*

If not—let it go.

5. Movement as Meditation

Do 10 minutes of mindful movement daily (stretching, walking, martial flow).

The goal: presence, not performance.

Weekly Action Steps

Day	Focus Area	Action Example
Monday	Mind Clarity	Journal your top 3 values & align your day
Tuesday	Body Discipline	20 mins of intentional movement
Wednesday	Emotional Mastery	Pause before reacting—breathe and observe
Thursday	Expression	Share your truth with someone or in art
Friday	Reflection	Review your week: what grew? what slipped?
Saturday	Decluttering	Remove one unnecessary thing from your life
Sunday	Recalibration	Plan your week aligned with your purpose

Your "Bruce Lee Way" Declaration

Write your own version of the following statement:

"I commit to living a life of clarity, courage, and truth. I will practice daily mastery, express my real self, and serve the world by becoming fully me. I am not here to impress—I am here to evolve. This is my way."

Reread it every morning. Live it every evening.

Final Encouragement

"Be water, my friend."

Yes—but also be fire, wind, and stone when needed.

Bruce was many things: strong and soft, disciplined and playful, fierce and gentle.

So are you.

Let your journal be your dojo.

Let your actions be your art.

Let your life be your legacy

14.2 Creating Your Own Philosophy of Living

Why You Need Your Own Philosophy

Most people live by default—repeating routines, beliefs, and patterns without asking:

"Is this truly *mine*?"

Bruce Lee refused to live on autopilot. He questioned everything—traditions, techniques, systems, and even himself.

And through that questioning, he created his own unique philosophy of living.

He called it Jeet Kune Do in martial arts.

But in life? It was simply living with awareness and truth.

What Is a Personal Life Philosophy?

It's your inner compass—a set of principles that guide your:

- Choices

- Actions

- Reactions

- Relationships

- Purpose

It's not a script. It's a living system.

Something you build, test, revise, and evolve—just like Bruce did.

Bruce Lee's Personal Philosophy in 6 Principles

1. Truth over tradition

   Don't follow blindly. Ask: *Does this work for me—right now?*

2. Simplicity is clarity

   Cut the fluff. Keep what matters.

3. Directness beats perfection

    Don't wait to be ready. Move.

4. Flow with reality

    Adapt, evolve, stay fluid.

5. Self-expression is self-realization

    Your uniqueness is your power.

6. Life is meant to be *lived*, not controlled

    Be awake. Be alive. Be fully you.

Build Your Own: A Guided Framework

Let's help your readers build a simple personal philosophy using Bruce's approach.

Step 1: Absorb What Is Useful

- What lessons, values, and tools from Bruce—or others— feel true to *you*?

- List your top 5 guiding beliefs right now.

Step 2: Discard What Is Not

- What habits, ideas, or expectations no longer serve you?

- Write down 3 things you're ready to let go of.

Step 3: Add What Is Uniquely Yours

- What gives you energy, joy, and meaning?

- What truth do you *feel*, even if the world doesn't validate it yet?

Now combine your answers into a short Life Code Statement—something like:

"I live with courage, simplicity, and compassion. I honor my truth, move with flow, and grow with intention. My path is mine—and I walk it awake."

Self-Reflections: Your Answer Please:

- *What do I believe about life, and why?*

- *What defines a good day for me—not by productivity, but by alignment?*

- *How do I want to treat others? How do I want to treat myself?*

- *What's worth fighting for in my world?*

- *Where in my life am I living by someone else's script?*

Practice: The Philosophy Check-In

Each week, ask yourself:

- Did I live according to my chosen values?

- Where did I drift off-course?

- What can I adjust, forgive, or recommit to?

Your philosophy is not a prison. It's a freedom map—to help you live more intentionally, not rigidly.

Insights:

Don't follow the path.

Follow your intention.

And let your footsteps become the path.

Bruce Lee's ultimate gift to us was not a martial art.

It was a mindset:

To question deeply.

To live simply.

To express fearlessly.

And to grow endlessly.

Now, it's your turn.

Craft your own way. Live by your own light.

And become unforgettable—by becoming fully, completely, uniquely you

My Story: My Growth Map Was Never Linear

Looking back, my growth journey was anything but smooth. It was chaotic, full of turns I never planned. But it was also real. And every step made me more *me*.

When I created the TRUE Growth Model, I realized I wasn't inventing a system—I was documenting what life had already taught me.

Like Bruce, I wasn't trying to fit into a mold. I was creating one through trial, practice, and reflection.

"Absorb what is useful, discard what is not, add what is uniquely your own."

That's the ultimate growth map. Yours. Your way. With awareness.

15. Bruce Lee Lives On: Modern Icons Inspired by Him

Bruce Lee's impact transcended generations, cultures, and disciplines. Though he passed away far too young, his influence is far from fading. Today, countless individuals, from athletes to entrepreneurs to artists, draw inspiration from his teachings. His philosophy of self-expression, discipline, and breaking boundaries has inspired a new wave of modern icons—people who embody his mindset in their own lives and work.

Bruce Lee's legacy is not just found in his martial arts prowess but in the way he challenged norms, expanded possibilities, and empowered others. His influence can be seen in the rise of figures who, like him, refuse to be confined by limits, continuously pushing the boundaries of their craft.

Key Modern Icons Inspired by Bruce Lee:

1. Conor McGregor: Fighting with the Mindset of a Champion

   Conor McGregor, one of the most famous mixed martial artists of this generation, embodies many of Bruce Lee's principles. McGregor has always praised Bruce Lee for his innovative approach to combat and for being a trailblazer. He has embraced Lee's philosophy of fighting as an art rather than just a sport, blending different styles to create his own unique approach.

o Mental strength: McGregor channels Lee's mindset of self-belief and preparation, focusing on both mental and physical training.

o Innovation: Like Bruce Lee, McGregor refuses to be bound by traditional rules and constantly seeks new ways to elevate his craft.

2. Kobe Bryant: The Mamba Mentality

The late Kobe Bryant, one of the greatest basketball players of all time, often spoke of Bruce Lee as an inspiration. Kobe's Mamba Mentality—his relentless drive for perfection, his passion for continuous growth, and his dedication to his craft—echoes Bruce Lee's emphasis on discipline, self-mastery, and never-ending improvement.

o Consistent improvement: Kobe modeled his life after Lee's approach of daily practice and growth, whether on the court or in his personal life.

o Philosophy of mastery: Much like Bruce Lee, Bryant rejected shortcuts to success, instead focusing on long-term effort and personal mastery.

3. Jet Li: Martial Arts as Philosophy

Martial artist and actor Jet Li has long been inspired by Bruce Lee, especially Lee's vision of martial arts as a way of life, not just fighting. Li has worked to expand the global appreciation of martial arts, blending traditional Chinese disciplines with modern techniques, much in the same way Bruce Lee did.

o Martial arts as self-expression: Li, like Lee, emphasizes the importance of martial arts as a philosophical practice, not just a physical skill.

o Bridging cultures: Both Li and Lee sought to bridge cultures and connect people through the universal language of martial arts.

4. Michelle Yeoh: Breaking Barriers in Film

Actress Michelle Yeoh has been a powerful force in breaking down racial and gender barriers in Hollywood, following in Bruce Lee's footsteps. Like Lee, Yeoh has continuously challenged stereotypes, showing the world that people of Asian descent can take center stage in action films and beyond.

- o Cultural impact: Yeoh has carried Bruce Lee's legacy into the modern era by showing that strong, multi-dimensional characters can emerge from diverse backgrounds.

- o Empowerment: Yeoh's career is a testament to Lee's teachings of self-empowerment and challenging societal limitations.

5. Joe Rogan: Championing Self-Mastery and Growth

As a martial artist, podcast host, and cultural influencer, Joe Rogan often speaks about the influence Bruce Lee has had on him. Rogan embodies Lee's philosophy of constant self-improvement and mental toughness in his approach to life, both in his career and personal growth.

- o Holistic development: Rogan advocates for the importance of mental clarity, physical fitness, and psychological toughness, aligning closely with Bruce Lee's principles.

- o Constant learning: Rogan's career path—spanning comedy, podcasting, and mixed martial arts commentary—reflects Lee's emphasis on being a lifelong learner and adapting to new challenges.

6. Ronda Rousey: Martial Arts Meets Personal Growth

Former UFC champion Ronda Rousey has been a vocal advocate of Bruce Lee's teachings, particularly his philosophy of mental strength and resilience. Rousey's meteoric rise in MMA was fueled by her focus on self-discipline and fighting with purpose, both of which are deeply rooted in Bruce Lee's ideology.

o Focus on mental toughness: Rousey has said that Bruce Lee's mindset helped her conquer self-doubt and overcome obstacles in her career.

o Breaking barriers: Just like Bruce Lee broke into Hollywood as an Asian actor, Rousey broke into the male-dominated world of mixed martial arts.

Bruce Lee's Enduring Legacy:

Bruce Lee didn't just create a legacy within martial arts; he created a philosophy of life that continues to influence artists, athletes, entrepreneurs, and leaders across the globe. From his philosophy of self-expression to his breakthrough approach to martial arts, Lee's ideas remain timeless and universally applicable. His teachings go beyond fighting—he taught the world how to live with authenticity, **

15.1 Living the Way: Modern Legends Who Embody Bruce Lee's Spirit

Bruce Lee didn't leave just teachings—

He left a living philosophy that echoes in the way certain people train, create, lead, and live.

This chapter is a celebration of that echo—a look at those who, knowingly or unknowingly, carry forward the essence of Bruce's way of life.

Kobe Bryant – The Mamba Mentality

Kobe studied Bruce Lee deeply. He once said,

"The way Bruce moved, thought, and trained—I built that into my own mindset."

Like Bruce, Kobe believed in:

- Daily discipline over sudden greatness

- Flowing around obstacles, not complaining about them

- Turning pain into performance

His famous "Mamba Mentality" was Bruce Lee's philosophy in a basketball jersey.

Jocko Willink – Discipline Equals Freedom

Former Navy SEAL, author, and leadership coach Jocko Willink channels Bruce's spirit through his mantra:

"Discipline equals freedom."

He wakes up at 4:30 AM. Trains daily.

Focuses on self-leadership first.

He teaches:

- Adaptability

- Ownership

- Simplicity in execution

- All traits Bruce practiced deeply.

Elon Musk – Breaking the System to Build Better

Musk is controversial, but one thing is clear:

He doesn't follow conventional rules.

He discards what doesn't work (like Bruce did with traditional martial forms) and invents his own way—whether in rockets, cars, or AI.

His approach mirrors Bruce's:

- Challenge norms

- Focus on truth, not tradition

- Move fast, fail forward

Prince – Pure Self-Expression

Prince, the musical genius, lived Bruce Lee's idea of "honestly expressing yourself."

He:

- Refused to be categorized

- Played 27 instruments

- Changed his name, his look, his sound—at will

- Maintained fierce control over his art

He didn't fit in. He stood out.

Not for fame, but for truth.

Just like Bruce.

Jay Shetty – Blending East and West Mindfully

Former monk turned global thought leader, Jay Shetty brings ancient wisdom into modern life.

He speaks about:

- Intentional living

- Inner clarity

- Detaching from ego

His content reaches millions, blending East and West philosophy—just as Bruce Lee did.

Tim Ferriss – Self-Experimentation and Mastery

Tim Ferriss, author of *The 4-Hour Workweek*, mirrors Bruce's obsession with:

- Efficiency

- Self-testing

- Continuous refinement

He studies himself in real-time—just like Bruce did with his mind, body, and habits.

He breaks things down, simplifies, and shares with the world—distilling wisdom into actionable tools.

Nipsey Hussle – The Marathon of Mastery

Rapper and entrepreneur Nipsey Hussle and Bruce Lee share notable parallels in their philosophies and approaches to personal development. He spoke often of:

- Ownership

- Purpose-driven living

- Long-term vision over instant success

He built businesses in his own neighborhood, staying authentic to his roots—Bruce's principle of staying real and serving others in action.

Common Traits of These Bruce Lee–Inspired Modern Icons

Trait	Expression Example
Authenticity	Prince's genre-defying creativity
Discipline	Kobe's relentless daily grind
Philosophical depth	Jay Shetty's mindful teachings

Efficiency	Tim Ferriss's lifestyle design
Adaptability	Elon Musk's industry disruption
Service	Nipsey's community leadership
Resilience	Jocko's mental toughness

Each of them, in their own field, asks:

"What is my way—and how do I live it fully?"

That's Bruce Lee's spirit. That's the invitation to all of us.

Reflection Prompt for the Reader

Who inspires me—not because they're famous, but because they live with truth and mastery?

How can I carry forward Bruce Lee's spirit in my own career, art, business, or relationships?

15.2 You as the Next Torchbearer

Bruce Lee didn't want you to become *him*.

He wanted you to become yourself—fully, fearlessly, and with fire.

He was a master not because he knew all the answers,

but because he never stopped asking, questioning, exploring, refining, evolving.

He built his body like a weapon.

He trained his mind like a monk.

He moved through life like water.

And most importantly, he lit a torch.

A torch that has now... been passed to you.

The Flame You Carry

You've read the stories.

You've felt the power of presence, discipline, simplicity, flow, and authenticity.

This isn't just a tribute to Bruce Lee.

This is a transformation of you.

And now, the question is simple:

What will you do with the fire?

Being Bruce in Your Own Life

You don't need to fight in tournaments.

You don't need to star in films.

You don't need a black belt.

But you *do* need:

- The courage to express yourself.

- The commitment to your practice.

- The honesty to face your fears.

- The humility to keep evolving.

That's the real martial art. That's the way of no way.

Start Where You Are

- Make your morning a dojo—train your mind and body with intention.

- Make your relationships a mirror—practice presence and truth.

- Make your work your art—bring excellence to even the smallest task.

- Make your life your masterpiece—refined not by perfection, but by progress.

Your Legacy Starts Now

You don't have to be famous to make an impact.

You just have to be real.

Consistent. Conscious. Caring.

Like Bruce.

The ripple starts with you:

- The way you walk into a room.

- The way you handle conflict.

- The way you treat your body, your time, your truth.

This is your practice.

This is your path.

This is your chance to carry the torch forward.

Final Reflection: Your Torchbearer Declaration

"I am the architect of my own life.

I live with presence.

I express my truth.

I grow with discipline.

I serve with strength and simplicity.

I am the next torchbearer."

Write it.

Speak it.

Live it.

Torchbearer's Journal Prompt

What does being a torchbearer mean to me?

- What will I stand for from this day forward?

- What small daily act will keep my flame alive?

- Who will feel more free, more brave, more awake—because I chose to live fully?

One Step at a Time

Bruce Lee said:

"Knowing is not enough, we must apply. Willing is not enough, we must do."

Now it's your time.

Not to follow. But to lead.

Not to copy. But to create.

This is not the end of a book.

This is the beginning of your own way.

Light the torch.

And walk forward—with fire, with flow, with freedom.

APPENDIX

Bruce Lee Quotes by Theme

A treasure chest of clarity, courage, and consciousness

Self-Expression & Authenticity

"Always be yourself, express yourself, have faith in yourself. Do not go out and look for a successful personality and duplicate it."

"The key to immortality is first living a life worth remembering."

"To express oneself honestly, not lying to oneself—that, my friend, is very hard to do."

Mindfulness & Presence

"Be water, my friend."

"Empty your mind. Be formless, shapeless—like water."

"The moment is freedom. I couldn't live by a rigid schedule. I try to live freely from moment to moment."

Discipline & Mastery

"I fear not the man who has practiced 10,000 kicks once, but I fear the man who has practiced one kick 10,000 times."

"If you love life, don't waste time, for time is what life is made of."

"The successful warrior is the average man, with laser-like focus."

Philosophy & Inner Clarity

"Absorb what is useful, discard what is not, add what is uniquely your own."

"A wise man can learn more from a foolish question than a fool can learn from a wise answer."

"The more we value things, the less we value ourselves."

Resilience & Overcoming Obstacles

"Do not pray for an easy life, pray for the strength to endure a difficult one."

"In the middle of chaos lies opportunity."

"Mistakes are always forgivable if one has the courage to admit them."

Adaptability & Fluid Thinking

"Be like water making its way through cracks. Do not be assertive, but adjust to the object, and you shall find a way around or through it."

"All fixed set patterns are incapable of adaptability or pliability. The truth is outside of all fixed patterns."

Purpose & Personal Growth

"A goal is not always meant to be reached; it often serves simply as something to aim at."

"Knowing is not enough; we must apply. Willing is not enough; we must do."

"To hell with circumstances; I create opportunities."

Legacy & Leadership

"The function and duty of a quality human being is the sincere and honest development of one's potential."

"If you don't want to slip up tomorrow, speak the truth today."

"Real living is living for others."

Resources & Further Exploration

Expand your journey beyond these pages

To deepen your journey into the teachings, philosophy, and life of Bruce Lee — and to support your own path of authentic growth — here are some carefully selected resources:

Recommended Books and Films

Books by Bruce Lee (and from his writings)

1. *Tao of Jeet Kune Do –*

    A philosophical and practical guide to Bruce's personal martial art, written during his recovery from injury.

Insight into movement, mindset, and martial truth.

2. *Striking Thoughts: Bruce Lee's Wisdom for Daily Living –*

    Over 800 of Bruce's personal thoughts and quotes organized by theme.

A practical philosophy for modern life.

3. *Bruce Lee: Artist of Life –*

    A collection of essays, letters, and interviews reflecting his views on life, self-expression, and creativity.

4. *Jeet Kune Do: Bruce Lee's Commentaries on the Martial Way –*

    Notes and annotations compiled by students and historians based on his training methods.

Books About Bruce Lee

5. *Bruce Lee: A Life* by Matthew Polly –

The definitive biography—deeply researched and vividly written.

Raw, real, and inspiring.

6. *The Warrior Within* by John Little –

Explores Bruce's core beliefs and how they can apply to your life.

Especially great for personal development readers.

7. *Bruce Lee: The Celebrated Life of the Golden Dragon* by John Little –

A visually rich tribute filled with rare photos and personal stories.

Books on Philosophy & Flow (Inspired by Bruce's Way)

8. *The Inner Game of Tennis* by W. Timothy Gallwey –

A classic on performance, mindfulness, and the battle between ego and presence.

9. *The Art of Learning* by Josh Waitzkin –

A modern-day warrior's journey—reflects Bruce's principles of mastery, adaptation, and resilience.

10. *Flow: The Psychology of Optimal Experience* by Mihaly Csikszentmihalyi –

Understand the mental state Bruce aimed for in training and in life

Philosophical Influences & Related Works

11. *Think on These Things* – J. Krishnamurti

On awareness, self-discovery, and freedom — a major influence on Bruce's thought.

12. *The Way of Zen* – Alan Watts

Understanding non-duality, fluid thought, and presence — principles echoed in Bruce's teachings.

13. *The War of Art* – Steven Pressfield

A powerful guide to resistance, mastery, and authentic living — aligned with Bruce Lee's life philosophy.

Must-Watch Bruce Lee Films

(For inspiration, cinematic flair, and storytelling)

1. *The Big Boss* (1971) – Bruce's first major film; a story of justice, strength, and awakening. Watch not just for the action — but for the metaphors behind every move.

2. *Fist of Fury* (1972) – Touches on themes of cultural pride, resistance, and moral courage.

3. *The Way of the Dragon* (1972) – Written, directed, and starred in by Bruce. Features his iconic fight with Chuck Norris.

4. *Enter the Dragon* (1973) – His most famous and last completed film. Combines philosophy, martial arts, and international appeal.

5. *Bruce Lee: A Warrior's Journey* (2000) – A documentary featuring never-before-seen footage and the uncompleted scenes from *Game of Death*.

Modern Documentaries & Interpretations

6. *Be Water* (2020, ESPN 30 for 30 series) –

A poetic documentary that weaves Bruce's personal story with broader themes of identity, racism, and rebellion.

Highly recommended for cultural context and emotion.

7. *I Am Bruce Lee* (2012) –

   Features commentary from athletes, actors, and thought leaders on how Bruce changed the world.

8. *The Legend of Bruce Lee* (TV series) –

   A dramatized version of Bruce's life story; good for those who prefer narrative over nonfiction.

Audio & Podcasts

- *The Bruce Lee Podcast* – by Shannon Lee & The Bruce Lee Foundation

- Conversations on how Bruce Lee's ideas apply to modern challenges and personal growth.

Websites & Online Archives

- BruceLee.com

- The official Bruce Lee site, offering philosophies, writings, and modern reflections curated by the Bruce Lee Foundation.

- Bruce Lee Foundation https://bruceleefoundation.org/

- Educational resources, events, and community projects inspired by Bruce's legacy.

Use these resources to continue your practice of being like water — adaptable, powerful, and true to yourself.

Timeline of Bruce Lee's Life

A journey of spirit, struggle, and self-mastery

1940 – Birth

- Nov 27, 1940 – Born in San Francisco, California, during the Hour of the Dragon (6:00 AM) in the Year of the Dragon.

Symbolically powerful beginning for someone destined to breathe fire into the world.

1941–1958 – Early Years in Hong Kong

- Raised in Hong Kong in a theatrical family; his father was a Cantonese opera star.

- Age 6 – Begins acting in films as a child actor.

- Teen years – Becomes involved in street fights and gang activities.

- Learns Wing Chun under the legendary Ip Man to defend himself and develop discipline.

1959 – Return to America

- Sent back to the U.S. by his parents to escape violence and seek better education.

- Settles in Seattle, works in a restaurant, and finishes high school.

- Begins teaching martial arts informally to friends and students.

1961–1964 – College & Jeet Kune Do Origins

- Enrolls at the University of Washington, studies philosophy and drama.

- Starts to develop his own martial art style—eventually called Jeet Kune Do (The Way of the Intercepting Fist).

- 1964 – Marries Linda Emery.

- Demonstrates martial arts at the Long Beach International Karate Championships—this catches the attention of Hollywood.

1965–1969 – Breaking into Hollywood

- Birth of son Brandon Lee (1965).

- Appears as Kato in *The Green Hornet* (1966–67)—his breakout U.S. TV role.

- Struggles with discrimination in Hollywood; limited to sidekick roles or stereotypical characters.

- Opens martial arts schools in Seattle, Oakland, and Los Angeles.

1970–1971 – Injury & Inner Awakening

- Suffers a serious back injury during training—told he may never kick again.

- During recovery, he writes and reflects deeply—this is when much of *Tao of Jeet Kune Do* is compiled.

- *This period becomes a spiritual rebirth, a turning inward that would define his philosophy.*

1971–1973 – Global Stardom in Hong Kong Cinema

- Returns to Hong Kong and becomes a martial arts superstar.

- Films:

  o *The Big Boss* (1971)

- o *Fist of Fury* (1972)

- o *The Way of the Dragon* (1972) – wrote, directed, starred

- o Begins work on *Game of Death*

- o *Enter the Dragon* (1973) – Hollywood-Hong Kong co-production, released posthumously

July 20, 1973 – Death

- Dies suddenly at age 32 in Hong Kong.

- Cause of death officially ruled as cerebral edema.

His death shocked the world, but his spirit exploded into legend.

Posthumous Impact

- *Enter the Dragon* becomes a global phenomenon.

- His daughter Shannon Lee and the Bruce Lee Foundation continue his legacy.

- His writings, teachings, and persona influence generations of athletes, philosophers, creators, and seekers of truth.

Legacy Lives On

Bruce Lee's life was short in years but vast in impact. He transformed:

- The way martial arts were perceived

- How Asians were represented in cinema

- The mindset of millions who seek to live with power, purpose, and presence

Acknowledgements

This book is a tribute not only to Bruce Lee's legacy but to every soul who dares to live authentically, rise through adversity, and express their truth without apology.

First and foremost, I offer my deepest gratitude to Bruce Lee, whose life was not just one of action and speed, but of thought, reflection, and relentless pursuit of inner mastery. Your philosophy, presence, and spirit continue to guide generations—including this humble student.

To the Bruce Lee Foundation and Shannon Lee, thank you for protecting and expanding Bruce's vision in the modern world. Your work keeps his fire alive.

To my teachers, mentors, and well-wishers who've walked beside me in silence and strength, thank you for whispering clarity when the world became noisy. Your unseen support shaped this journey.

To my readers and fellow seekers—engineers, artists, leaders, dreamers—this book was written for you. May Bruce's energy awaken your own. You are not just a reader of this book; you are its continuation.

To my family and friends, your patience and love created the stillness in which this book could be born.

I must acknowledge the pivotal role of Technology and AI tools like ChatGPT in shaping this book and accelerating its publication. These innovations have been invaluable thinking partners, refining my ideas, enhancing my expression, and making the journey of bringing this book to life both efficient and enriching.

Above all, I express my deepest gratitude to the universal power that signalled my intellect to embark on this journey. Without this predesigned guidance, this book would not have been possible.

And finally, to every obstacle, injury, failure, and delay—you were all sacred training grounds. Just as Bruce taught us, you helped me "be like water"—to bend, to move, to flow, and to become.

This book is not an ending, but a ripple in the vast ocean of becoming.

With deep respect and boundless energy,

Pradeepkumar K Padmanabhan

ABOUT THE AUTHOR

Pradeepkumar K Padmanabhan

Pradeepkumar K Padmanabhan (Capt. Pradeepkumar KP, Retd.) is a former Indian Army Officer, experienced Engineer, Techpreneur, and passionate Engineers' Growth Coach. From his service as a Technical Officer in the Indian Army to leading multiple entrepreneurial ventures, his journey has been defined by leadership, innovation, and impact.

Now, his true calling is empowering engineers—helping them build purpose-driven careers, achieve financial success, and create a balanced life.

Pradeepkumar is on a mission to empower 100,000 engineers to grow holistically—professionally, personally, and spiritually. With over 30 years of experience in engineering and leadership, he has walked the path of rigorous self-discipline, introspection, and purposeful living.

Deeply inspired by ancient wisdom, modern psychology, and legends like Bruce Lee, Pradeepkumar blends clarity, courage, and consciousness into everything he teaches. He believes that sustainable success is rooted in authenticity, daily practices, and the unshakable will to evolve.

He is the author of *Automate Your Growth* and *Engineers' Growth Redefined*, and a firm believer in building a resilient society—starting with individuals who are aligned, self-aware, and mission-driven.

This book is part of his deeper calling—to inspire you not just to admire Bruce Lee, but to apply his spirit in your own journey of mastery, meaning, and contribution.

DISCLAIMER

The information provided in this book is for general informational purposes only. While every effort has been made to ensure the accuracy and reliability of the content at the time of publication, the author and publisher make no representations or warranties of any kind, express or implied, about the completeness, accuracy, or suitability of the information contained herein for any purpose.

This book is not intended to serve as a substitute for professional advice, including but not limited to legal, medical, financial, or other specialized guidance. Readers are encouraged to consult with qualified professionals regarding their specific circumstances before making decisions based on the information in this book.

The opinions expressed in this book are those of the author and do not necessarily reflect the views of the publisher or any other affiliated parties. Any references to real events, people, or entities are included for illustrative purposes and should not be interpreted as endorsements or definitive statements of fact.

The author and publisher shall not be liable for any loss, damage, or inconvenience arising from the use of, or reliance on, the information contained in this book. By reading this book, you acknowledge that you assume full responsibility for your actions and decisions based on its content.

MAY I ASK YOU FOR A SMALL FAVOR?

First, I want to thank you for reading this book. You could have chosen any other book, but you took mine, and I appreciate this. I hope you have at least a few actionable insights that will positively impact your daily life.

Can I ask for 30 seconds more of your time?

I'd love it if you could leave a review of the book. That will help me grow my readership by encouraging folks to take a chance on my books.

Keeping it straight - reviews are the lifeblood of any author.

It will take less than a minute of your time but will tremendously help me reach out to more people.

If you liked this book, please consider posting an honest review on your preferred retailer. And I'd love to see your review. Thanks for your support.

9 798899 291449